The
Catholic
Kids'
Cookbook

Published by Word on Fire Votive, an imprint of
Word on Fire, Elk Grove, IL 60007
© 2024 by Word on Fire Catholic Ministries
Printed in Italy

Cover design, typesetting, and interior art direction by Nicolas Fredrickson and Clare Sheaf
Food styling by Clare Sheaf, Haley Stewart, and Marisa Fredrickson
Photography by Clare Sheaf

ISBN: 978-1-68578-168-2

Library of Congress Control Number: 2024934728

HALEY STEWART

CLARE SHEAF

The Catholic Kids' Cookbook

HOLY DAYS AND HEAVENLY FOOD

WORD ON FIRE

To Daniel, Benjamin, Lucy, Gwen, and
Hildie: you are my favorite chefs. —H.S.

To my husband, Jacob, and his culinary
amnesia: for always proclaiming each recipe I
cook him to be "the best meal he's ever had";
to my newborn daughter, Annie: I cannot
wait to live liturgically with you! —C.S.

Contents

WHAT IS THE LITURGICAL YEAR?   8

LITURGICAL SEASONS AND COLORS   10

THE LITURGICAL YEAR TIMELINE   12

HOW DO WE LIVE LITURGICALLY?   14

WHO ARE THE SAINTS?   16

HOW TO USE THIS BOOK   18

Advent

24   *Happy New Year!*

26   ST. ANDREW (NOVEMBER 30)
    Fisherman's Breakfast

30   FIRST SUNDAY OF ADVENT
    Cozy Advent Chili

34   ST. NICHOLAS (DECEMBER 6)
    St. Nicholas' Chocolate Dowries
    Orange Pomanders

42   THE IMMACULATE CONCEPTION (DECEMBER 8)
    Our Lady's Fig Tarts

46   OUR LADY OF GUADALUPE (DECEMBER 12)
    Guadalupe Hot Chocolate

50   ST. LUCY (DECEMBER 13)
    Eyes of St. Lucy (Lemon Posset)

Christmas

56   *Joy to the World!*

58   THE NATIVITY (DECEMBER 25)
    Manger Munchies

64   ST. STEPHEN (DECEMBER 26)
    Yuletide Garland

70   ST. MACARIUS (JANUARY 2)
    St. Macarius' Sparkling Sugar Plums

74   EPIPHANY
    King Cake

Ordinary Time

84   *A Time to Grow*

86   ST. BRIGID (FEBRUARY 1)
    St. Brigid's Endless Herbed Butter

88   ST. PAUL MIKI (FEBRUARY 6)
    Miki's Maki

Lent

96 *Prepare Your Hearts*

98 **SHROVE TUESDAY**
Shrovetide Pancakes

100 **ASH WEDNESDAY**
Ash Wednesday Common Bread

104 **ST. JOSEPH (MARCH 19)**
Zeppole di San Giuseppe

110 **THE ANNUNCIATION (MARCH 25)**
Gabriel's Wings Alfredo

114 *Holy Week*

116 **GOOD FRIDAY**
Good Friday Potato and Leek Soup

120 **HOLY SATURDAY**
Hot Cross Buns

Easter

124 *New Life in Christ*

126 **EASTER SUNDAY**
Easter Edible Flower Salad

132 **ST. GEORGE (APRIL 23)**
St. George's Dragon Eggs

138 **ST. CATHERINE OF SIENA (APRIL 29)**
St. Catherine's Fiery Tomato Risotto

142 **THE ASCENSION**
Ascension Clouds

146 **PENTECOST**
Le Colombier Dove Cake

Ordinary Time

156 *More Time to Grow*

158 **TRINITY SUNDAY**
Trinity Chicken Pot Pie

162 **NATIVITY OF ST. JOHN THE BAPTIST (JUNE 24)**
St. John the Baptist's Wild Honey Cake

168 **BL. PIER GIORGIO FRASSATI (JULY 4)**
To the Heights Trail Mix

172 **ST. CHARBEL MAKHLOUF (JULY 24)**
St. Charbel's Spicy Smashed Potatoes

174 **ST. HILDEGARD OF BINGEN (SEPTEMBER 17)**
St. Hildegard's Cheerful Cookies

178 **THE ARCHANGELS (SEPTEMBER 29)**
St. Michael's Blackberry Crumble

184 **ST. THÉRÈSE OF LISIEUX (OCTOBER 1)**
St. Thérèse's Favorite Chocolate Eclairs

190 *Hallowtide*

192 **ALL SOULS (NOVEMBER 2)**
Soul Cakes

198 **CHRIST THE KING**
Christ the King Breakfast Crowns

IT BEGINS AGAIN	202
ABOUT	206
ACKNOWLEDGEMENTS	207
REFERENCES	208

ARTWORK
Johannes Vermeer
Christ in the House of Martha and Mary
c. 1655

What Is the Liturgical Year?

Every family has traditions. Your family sings a certain song on birthdays. You gather around the table to share special meals. You look at photographs of favorite memories. When you are all together to celebrate, you might hear stories about the day you were born or an important tale from your parents' or grandparents' lives. These shared traditions help you to remember who you are and to understand your story.

The Church is a family too. And it's a family with traditions: songs, meals, prayers, and celebrations. These traditions remind us who we are. They help us tell our story, and it's a very beautiful story: we are loved by God and he made us part of his family.

To tell this important tale, the Church gives us a special gift: the liturgical year (sometimes called the Christian Year). The liturgical year is the calendar of seasons, feasts, and fasts by which we learn the story of God's love for us.

Living liturgically means making this holy calendar our own. We get to participate in God's great story! If you've ever been in a Christmas pageant or Nativity play as an angel or a shepherd, you helped tell a story we all know well: the story of when Jesus was born. Even though this event happened many years ago, we still celebrate Christmas every year. God's gift of Jesus changed everything. Because this story is so important, we return to it again and again. By living liturgically, we retell the story of Christmas and the other important moments in the history of the Church. We are all invited into this great story.

Liturgical Seasons and Colors

The Christian Year follows several liturgical seasons that help us walk through the story of God's love for us. We journey through these times together with our brothers and sisters in Christ. There are many things that can help us remember which season we are in and what that season means.

The priest's vestments—the garments that he wears to celebrate the Mass—will be the color of the season (or holy day being observed) to help remind us of the liturgical year. As we dive into recipes, we'll talk more about what each season signifies, but here's a quick guide to the liturgical colors:

PURPLE

Purple is the color we use for Advent, the season observed during the four weeks leading up to Christmas. This color represents preparation, as we get ready to celebrate the Nativity, when Christ was born as a baby to the Blessed Virgin Mary. We must prepare for Christmas during this time!

Purple is also used during Lent, the season of forty days that prepares us for Easter. During this time, we focus on penitence—feeling sorrow for times when we failed to love and obey God, and asking for his forgiveness.

WHITE

Christmas and Easter are the highest holy days of the year and are celebrated with the color white. Christmas Day celebrates the Nativity, when Jesus was born, but the season of Christmas lasts for several days (great news if you like to celebrate). Easter is the most important day of the liturgical year, and it begins a festive season that lasts for fifty days.

RED

Red is used for the Passion of Christ as well as Pentecost, the birthday of the Church when the Holy Spirit descended on the followers of Jesus. It is also used to honor martyrs who died for their faith.

GREEN

Ordinary Time, the weeks after Christmas leading up to Lent and the weeks following Pentecost leading up to Advent, is marked with the color green. Just as we see green plants growing in the sunshine, the green of Ordinary Time is a reminder that this season is a time for our faith to grow.

The beginning and ending date of different liturgical seasons can change from year to year but this timeline will give you a general idea of where each season falls.

The
Liturgical
Year
Timeline

ADVENT
(Beginning of the Liturgical Year)

CHRISTMAS

ORDINARY TIME

LENT

HOLY WEEK

EASTER

ORDINARY TIME

How Do We Live Liturgically?

The Bible tells us to "pray without ceasing" (1. Thess. 5:17). But how do we do this? Our days are filled with school, friends, family, sports, music, activities, and chores. We are busy! We don't live in quiet monasteries like monks and nuns. Life in our houses might be very loud. How can we pray without ceasing?

Sometimes when we pray, we speak to God by repeating words that have been passed down to us like the "Hail Mary" or the "Our Father." Our hands may be folded and our eyes closed as we think about the words and offer them to God. But that isn't the only way that prayer can fill our lives. If we know that prayer is simply "the raising of one's mind and heart to God" (*Catechism of the Catholic Church* 255) then the call to pray at all times makes more sense. There are many ways to raise our minds and hearts to God! Can cooking a meal and sharing it with family and friends be a form of prayer? It certainly can. We call this living liturgically. We can celebrate feast days. We can offer certain sacrifices to God during times of penance. We can remember the saints in heaven and their holy lives. Living liturgically is a kind of prayer because we are lifting our minds and hearts to God together with the rest of God's family, the Church.

There are many ways to observe those holy days and seasons: music, celebrations, special liturgies, and, of course, food! In this book, we want to share some ideas for how you can participate in the liturgical year with your family by cooking delicious recipes that will help you remember the great story of God's love.

Who Are the Saints?

Many of the recipes in this book refer to certain saints of the Church and can be made to celebrate their feast days. The saints are holy men and women who shine with the love of Christ. They show us how to live faithful lives, they pray for us, and they cheer us on to glory. The saints want to help us get to heaven, and by honoring them and learning their stories, we can become more like them.

The Catholic Church has recognized *thousands* of saints through a process called canonization. That's far too many saints for any one family to celebrate, so just pick a few and you can join the Church in honoring and befriending them.

The calendar of saints is filled with warrior kings, gentle monks, moms, dads, children, teenagers, popes, farmers, rich people, poor people, brilliant scholars, and people who never learned how to read. The saints reflect God's love in many different ways: some were martyrs and others were teachers, some were called to religious life and others to marriage. But they all lived with heroic virtue, and we can look to them for inspiration and count on them for their prayers. You can use this cookbook to learn more about the saints and how to celebrate them.

CANONIZATION

The process by which the Church determines that someone is a saint and a model of heroic virtue to inspire Catholics all over the world.

ARTWORK
Albrecht Dürer
Adoration of the Trinity
1511

How to Use This Book

This cookbook contains thirty-three recipes to help you participate in the liturgical year. But keep in mind that these are just suggestions. The Church has only a few, simple rules about how Catholics must observe the liturgical year (such as attending Mass on Holy Days of Obligation or fasting on Ash Wednesday and Good Friday). For the most part, the way to honor special days in your home and family is up to you! There is no official Vatican checklist. There are many ways to live out the Christian Year and participate in the beautiful traditions of the Church and her holy days and saints.

Here are some important things to keep in mind when observing the liturgical year by cooking:

FEAST

A special meal or banquet for the celebration of a day that is set aside to honor Jesus, Mary, or a saint in a special way. Some feast days are also Holy Days of Obligation, days on which Catholics must attend Mass and refrain from unnecessary work.

FAST

Giving up a particular food or activity you enjoy as an act of penance so as to unite your sufferings with Christ and to prepare yourself physically and spiritually for a coming feast.

Using sharp knives, the oven, the stovetop, mixers, food processors, and blenders requires supervision by a grown-up.

Read the whole recipe ahead of time and make sure you have all the ingredients and supplies you need.

Some recipes are very simple and you can do them all by yourself. Other recipes are trickier, take more time to complete, and may need more help from a grown-up. To help you determine how difficult a recipe is, we've ranked each recipe Easy, Moderate, or Difficult.

Be aware of food allergies. If someone who may eat the food has a food allergy, be sure to have a grown-up check the ingredients of any recipe you are preparing.

Always wash your hands before preparing food (and wash them again anytime you touch raw eggs, meat, etc.).

Pay attention to how many people each recipe serves. If you come from a big family, you may need to double (or triple!) the recipe.

These recipes use measurements and temperatures that will be familiar to an American audience. If you are an international reader, you may need to convert Fahrenheit to Celsius, etc.

Show love for your family by taking time to clean up any messes you make!

Advent

O come, O come, Emmanuel,

and ransom captive Israel

that mourns in lonely exile here

until the Son of God appear.

ARTWORK
Léon Augustin Lhermitte
La prière, église Saint-Bonnet
1920

Happy New Year!

Have you ever asked to stay up until midnight on December 31st to celebrate the New Year on January 1st? It's exciting to begin a fresh new year. Would you be surprised if I told you that the Church's calendar has its own special new year? The new Christian Year begins on the First Sunday of Advent, which is the Sunday closest to St. Andrew's Day on November 30th. If you observe Advent, you can tell your family "Happy New Year!" on that first Sunday.

As the days are shortening and growing darker, Advent is the time when we watch for Jesus, the light of the world. We get our houses and our hearts ready for the arrival of the Christ Child. In fact, the word Advent means "the coming" because it's when we focus on the amazing moment when Jesus came to earth as a little baby.

We celebrate Advent as a season of waiting—just as Mary and Joseph patiently waited and prepared for the birth of baby Jesus. If you've ever welcomed a new baby into your family, whether a cousin or brother or sister, you know that there is a lot to do to prepare. Even though they had little to offer this new baby, Joseph and Mary would have prepared the manger with soft hay to comfort baby Jesus. We might not have much to offer Jesus in Advent, but we can prepare in small ways to show Jesus that we are readying our minds and hearts for his arrival.

During Advent, you might want to clean up your room and help your family tidy up the house so that it's ready for Christmas decorations. You might want to "tidy up" your soul by going to confession and spending time with Jesus in prayer. You can also play music for Advent that helps you think about preparing for Christmas. We all get excited for Christmas, but don't skip over the special season of Advent!

Fisherman's Breakfast

St. Andrew

ADVENT | NOVEMBER 30

● ◌ ◌ EASY

St. Andrew was a fisherman. He was a friend of Jesus and the brother of St. Peter, the first pope. St. Andrew wanted everyone to follow Jesus and accept God's love. He traveled as far north as the Black Sea to share the Gospel. Even the danger of being killed for his faith did not hold St. Andrew back from his mission, and he was eventually martyred in Greece.

Ancient sources say that when St. Andrew was martyred, he was bound (rather than nailed) to a cross. Sacred art shows St. Andrew on a cross raised in the shape of an X. This shape is called a St. Andrew's Cross and can be found on the flag of Scotland, where he is the patron saint.

To remember this connection to Scotland and honor St. Andrew's work as a fisherman, make this simple Scottish dish of smoked salmon and scrambled eggs for your family!

Note: We have included St. Andrew in the Advent section of the cookbook. Depending on which day of week Christmas falls, the First Sunday of Advent can occur anywhere between November 27 and December 3; as a result, St. Andrew's feast day sometimes falls at the end of Ordinary Time.

SERVES: 4

PREPARATION:
15 minutes

INGREDIENTS:
8 eggs
¼ cup milk or cream
Dash of salt and pepper
Pat (or small square) of butter
Bread for toast
2 ounces smoked salmon
Chives

SUPPLIES:
Pan or griddle for stovetop
Medium-sized bowl for mixing

1. Crack the eggs into a medium-sized bowl.

2. Add the milk or cream and a dash of salt and pepper.

3. Gently beat the eggs.

4. Melt a pat of butter in a pan over medium-low heat.

5. When melted, pour the eggs into the pan, stirring them often so that they don't burn on the bottom.

6. When the eggs are firm, remove to a plate and turn off the stovetop.

7. Toast your bread.

8. Serve the eggs with toast and a slice of smoked salmon on the side. Add the chives on top of your eggs in an "X" shape like a St. Andrew's Cross.

This beautiful prayer is traditionally prayed 15 times a day from St. Andrew's Day until Christmas Day.

Hail and blessed be the hour and moment in which the Son of God was born of the most pure Virgin Mary, at midnight, in Bethlehem, in the piercing cold. In that hour vouchsafe, I beseech thee, O my God, to hear my prayer and grant my desires through the merits of our Savior Jesus Christ, and of his Blessed Mother.

Amen.

Cozy Advent Chili

When the weather outside is chilly during the season of Advent, it's a great time to enjoy warm soups and stews. And making simple meals reminds us that the season of holiday celebration isn't quite here yet. If we eat simple food during Advent, then when Christmas comes, all the special holiday treats will make it feel like a real *feast*.

This recipe with a classic chili as a base is simple but fun to make because of all the toppings you can add to spice it up!

First Sunday of Advent
ADVENT

● ● ○ MODERATE

SERVES: 6–8

PREPARATION:
40 minutes

INGREDIENTS:
1 tablespoon olive oil

1 yellow onion, diced

1 pound ground beef

1½ tablespoons chili powder (you can add an extra tablespoon if you like spice)

2 tablespoons sugar

Pinch of cayenne pepper
(leave out if you don't like spice)

2 tablespoons ground cumin

1 tablespoon garlic powder

1 tablespoon onion powder

2 teaspoons salt

½ teaspoon pepper

2 tablespoons tomato paste

2 (15-ounce) cans kidney beans, drained

3 cups beef broth

1 (16-ounce) can diced tomatoes

1 (8-ounce) can tomato sauce

TOPPINGS:
Sour cream

Green onions (chopped)

Cilantro (chopped)

Fritos or tortilla chips

Shredded cheddar cheese

Shredded lettuce

SUPPLIES:
Large soup pot

Cozy Advent Chili (Continued)

1. Add olive oil to a large pot and heat over medium heat. Once heated, add diced onion and sauté until clear.

2. Add ground beef and brown for about 7 minutes. You'll want to stir the ground beef as it cooks to break it up into smaller pieces.

3. Add spices, sugar, salt, pepper, and tomato paste and combine.

4. Add kidney beans, beef broth, diced tomatoes, and tomato sauce and bring to a boil.

5. Turn down heat to low (or medium-low) and simmer for 25 minutes.

6. Turn off heat and let the chili cool for 10 minutes, then serve it into bowls.

7. Add whatever toppings you like!

St. Nicholas' Chocolate Dowries

St. Nicholas

ADVENT | DECEMBER 6

 EASY

In the midst of the Advent season, while we wait in silence for the birth of Christ, we have a little festive light—St. Nicholas' feast day! St. Nicholas of Myra was a fourth-century bishop remembered for his generosity and care for the poor. He discovered that a father didn't have enough money for his three daughters' dowries (money they needed in order to marry). St. Nicholas wanted to help the family but did not wish to humiliate them in public, so he came to the house at night and put the money in a purse to throw down the chimney. Some say the bag of money fell down the chimney and landed into the daughters' shoes that were drying by the fireplace. In honor of this story, some families put their shoes out by the fireplace the night before St. Nicholas' feast day in hopes that a little gift might be found the next morning.

Honor the legacy of St. Nicholas by making these chocolate-dipped "dowries"! The clementine represents the gold that St. Nicholas gave to the family, and the chocolate represents the purse covering the money.

SERVES: 5–8

PREPARATION:
15 minutes

INGREDIENTS:
5 clementines
1 cup semi-sweet chocolate chips
¼ cup coconut oil

SUPPLIES:
Wire rack
Microwave-safe bowl

1. Peel the clementines and separate the sections. Lay the sections out on a wire rack.

2. Melt the semi-sweet chocolate in the microwave in a microwave-safe bowl. It's easy to burn chocolate, so try heating it for 30 seconds (or less) at a time and stirring thoroughly until the chocolate is melted.

3. When the chocolate is fully melted, add the ¼ cup of coconut oil. Dip the sections of the clementines into the melted chocolate. The coconut oil will act as a "shell" and dry the chocolate quickly.

Orange Pomanders

While you're enjoying your chocolate dowries, have fun decorating orange pomanders. These pomanders aren't for eating; they're for adding fragrant color to your home.

St. Nicholas

ADVENT | DECEMBER 6

● ◐ ◯ EASY

INGREDIENTS:
Clementines
Whole cloves

1. The beauty of this craft is its simplicity: just pierce the oranges with cloves, decorating in whatever pattern you'd like—spirals, diamonds, stripes, etc.

2. Place the pomanders in a decorative bowl with evergreen branches, dried orange slices, cranberries, and pinecones for a festive centerpiece.

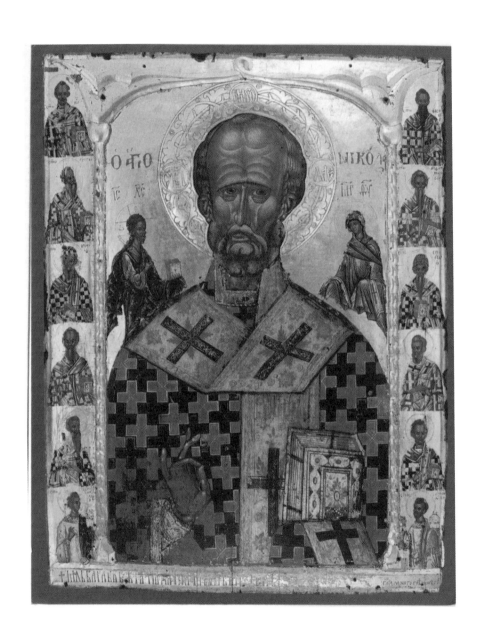

O good Saint Nicholas, you who are the joy of the children, put in my heart the spirit of childhood, of which the Gospel speaks, and teach me to seed happiness around me. You, whose feast prepares us for Christmas, open my faith to the mystery of God made man.

You, good bishop and shepherd, help me to find my place in the Church and inspire the Church to be faithful to the Gospel.

O good Saint Nicholas, patron of children, sailors, and the helpless, watch over those who pray to Jesus, your Lord and theirs, as well as over those who humble themselves before you. Bring us all in reverence to the Holy Child of Bethlehem, where true joy and peace are found.

Amen.

ARTWORK
Unknown
Icon of St. Nicholas the Wonderworker
FIFTEENTH CENTURY

Our Lady's Fig Tarts

The Immaculate Conception
ADVENT | DECEMBER 8

 **EASY**

The Immaculate Conception celebrates the day when Mary began to grow in the womb of her mother, St. Anne, nine months before we celebrate Mary's birthday on September 8th. God had a very special plan for Mary, his Blessed Mother. From the very beginning of her existence, she was holy and without the stain of original sin on her soul.

When you think of original sin, you might remember Adam and Eve, who ate the fruit that was forbidden to them by God in the Garden of Eden and passed on their sin to the rest of the human race. We don't know what fruit they ate, but some people think it could have been a fig because Adam and Eve clothed themselves with fig leaves after they sinned.

To celebrate the Immaculate Conception, we aspire to be holy like Mary, and we are grateful that God offers us Baptism so we can be free from the stain of original sin like Our Lady. Feast on this special day by making these delicious fig tarts!

SERVES: 8

PREPARATION:
25 minutes (plus 40 minutes to thaw the pastry)

INGREDIENTS:
1 package frozen puff pastry
4 tablespoons fig jam or preserves
4 ounces brie cheese
⅓ cup honey
Optional: fresh fruit

SUPPLIES:
Muffin tin

1. Remove your puff pastry from the freezer and let thaw for 40 minutes at room temperature.

2. Lightly grease a muffin tin.

3. Preheat oven to 400°F.

4. Unroll your packaged puff pastry and cut into 8 even squares. Place squares into the muffin tin.

5. Spread a layer of fig jam on the pastry.

6. Chop the brie into ½-inch cubes and distribute 2 to 3 cubes onto the center of each pastry.

7. Bake the pastries in the oven for 10 minutes.

8. Take out the pastries (they should be on their way to golden brown, but not quite) and drizzle them with honey before placing them back in the oven for another 5 minutes. Enjoy warm or cooled with fresh fruit on top!

"I am the Immaculate Conception."

—OUR LADY TO ST. BERNADETTE

ARTWORK
Sandro Botticelli
Madonna of the Magnificat
1481

Guadalupe Hot Chocolate

Our Lady of Guadalupe

ADVENT | DECEMBER 12

 EASY

The Feast of Our Lady of Guadalupe celebrates the story of Mary's appearance to St. Juan Diego—an indigenous man who lived in Mexico and converted to the Catholic faith. Juan Diego was such a strong believer that he walked fifteen miles each morning to daily Mass and fifteen miles home. It was on these walks that Our Lady appeared to him and entrusted him with the task of asking the local bishop to erect a church in her honor in the very hills that Juan Diego walked. When the bishop did not believe Juan Diego, Mary sent him (in the middle of winter) to gather roses from a hill to bring to the bishop. Juan Diego carried the roses in his tilma (cloak) and then dropped the beautiful flowers at the feet of the bishop. At that moment, on his tilma an image of Our Lady miraculously appeared! You can still see his tilma today in the Basilica of Our Lady of Guadalupe in Mexico City. In honor of this feast day, why not go on a Rosary walk and return home for a warm cup of this delicious hot chocolate?

Ancient civilizations in Mexico developed a special drink made of cocoa beans blended with other ingredients like vanilla or chilis. As chocolate became popular around the world, new ways to enjoy the delicious ingredient were invented. This recipe for hot chocolate will be creamy, sweet, and just a little bit spicy! (But if you are sensitive to spice, you can decrease the amount of chili powder and cayenne pepper, or even leave it out altogether.)

SERVES: 4

PREPARATION:
10 minutes

INGREDIENTS:
6 cups milk

2 teaspoons vanilla extract

4 tablespoons sugar

1 teaspoon cinnamon

⅛ teaspoon chili powder

⅛ teaspoon cayenne pepper

4 tablespoons cocoa powder

2 ounces bittersweet chocolate

Optional: whipped cream or marshmallows

SUPPLIES:
Saucepan

1. Add 1 cup of the milk to a large saucepan over medium heat. Whisk the milk as it warms. (You don't want it to burn.)

2. When the milk is warmed, add the vanilla, sugar, cinnamon, chili powder, cayenne pepper, and cocoa powder and keep whisking.

3. When the milk mixture is smooth, add the bittersweet chocolate. Keep whisking until the chocolate has fully melted. It will take a while for all the chocolate to get warm and combine with the milk mixture.

4. Add the remaining milk and whisk until the texture is smooth.

5. Take off of heat and pour into mugs. Serve with a dollop of whipped cream or marshmallows, if desired!

"Am I not here, I who am your mother? Are you not under my shadow and protection? Am I not the source of your joy? Are you not in the hollow of my mantle, in the crossing of my arms?"

——OUR LADY OF GUADALUPE TO ST. JUAN DIEGO

ARTWORK
Nicolás Enríquez
*The Virgin of Guadalupe
with the Four Apparitions*
1773

Eyes of St. Lucy
(Lemon Posset)

St. Lucy

ADVENT | DECEMBER 13

● ● ● DIFFICULT

SERVES: 8

PREPARATION:
30 minutes (plus 4 hours cooling)

INGREDIENTS:
4 lemons
⅔ cup sugar
2 cups heavy cream

SUPPLIES:
2 saucepans
Zester

LUCY

The name "Lucy" or "Lucia" means "light."

St. Lucy was a young Christian woman who lived in Syracuse on the island of Sicily during the fourth century when Christians were persecuted by the Roman government. Lucy wanted to offer her life to Christ and refused to marry the pagan man chosen for her. She gave away the money saved for her dowry as a gift to the poor, and the man who wanted to marry her was furious! He told the governor that Lucy was secretly a Christian and he wanted her to be cruelly punished for her faith. But a strange thing happened: Lucy was miraculously protected from the governor's attempts to harm her. When he ordered soldiers to carry her away, she became heavy as a boulder and could not be moved. When they tried to burn her, she would not burn. They even tried to blind her, but God restored her sight. She was finally martyred for her faith, and we remember her bravery, generosity, and unwavering faith in God.

St. Lucy is often depicted in sacred images in a strange way: she's holding her own eyeballs on a plate! This is a reminder of God's miraculous way of restoring her eyesight. In honor of this miracle, make delicious lemon posset and serve in lemon rinds to look like St. Lucy's eyes.

1. Zest 2 lemons and set lemon zest aside.

2. Cut lemons in half longways. Squeeze the juice out of 4 lemon halves into a cup. If any seeds get into the juice, just remove them.

3. Remove the fruit from all the lemon halves. (You will use the rinds to serve the lemon posset.) This part is tricky. You may need a grown-up to help you get all the fruit out of the lemons. After removing the fruit, you can discard it or use it for another recipe.

4. Add the lemon juice, lemon zest, and sugar to a small saucepan and stir until combined.

5. Over medium-low heat, bring the saucepan to a simmer. Simmer for 5 minutes or until the sugar has melted and the liquid is syrupy. Remove from heat and set aside.

6. Add the cream to the other saucepan. Heat the cream until it simmers (or barely boils). You'll want to do this very slowly or else the cream will be the wrong texture. Once it starts to simmer, turn down the heat to low. It should simmer for 4 to 5 minutes; then take the saucepan off the heat.

7. Very slowly pour the lemon and sugar mixture into the cream, whisking constantly.

8. Put the lemon halves on a tray to avoid a mess, and pour the mixture into the lemon halves. The mixture will be hot, so you may need a grown-up's help. You will have some mixture left over, so pour it into small bowls. Let it cool. Once cooled to room temperature, move to the fridge overnight (or for at least 4 hours). Then grab a spoon and enjoy!

"Those whose hearts are pure are temples of the Holy Spirit."

—ST. LUCY

ARTWORK
Francesco del Cossa
Saint Lucy
c. 1473/1474

Christmas

Silent night! Holy night!

All is calm, all is bright

round yon virgin mother and child!

Holy infant, so tender and mild,

sleep in heavenly peace,

sleep in heavenly peace!

ARTWORK
Macmillan & Co
A Christmas Carol
1873

Joy to the World!

After the long wait of Advent, Christmas Day arrives with joy! The Christmas story is a familiar one: Joseph traveling to Bethlehem with pregnant Mary riding on a donkey; baby Jesus born in a stable because there was no room in the inn, laid in a feeding trough, and honored by shepherds and angels. You've probably been told this story your whole life, and it's easy to forget what a strange turn of events it is! The Mother of God had to ride on a donkey? The King of kings was born not in a palace but in a barn? Instead of announcing himself to the world as a strong and mighty warrior, God decided to be born like all of us as a little, helpless baby? The angels announced his birth to simple shepherds who were out watching their smelly sheep instead of first telling the wealthy nobles and lords of the land? The birth of Jesus is a glorious and strange surprise.

And Christmas begins not just one day of celebration but a whole festive season. You may have heard of the "Twelve Days of Christmas," which refers to the time between Christmas Day and the Feast of Epiphany (traditionally celebrated on January 6). Then, the Christmas season continues until the Feast of the Baptism of the Lord. So take the time to enjoy this season to the fullest!

Here are some ideas for observing this holy, happy season:

- Go to Mass with your family

- Make a popcorn and cranberry Yuletide garland to decorate your tree (instructions on page 64)

- Drive around to look at Christmas lights

- Sing Christmas carols with family and friends

- Watch a Christmas movie

- Make sugar plums (recipe on page 70)

Manger Munchies

On December 25th, we celebrate the Good News of Christmas: that Jesus Christ was born to the world! We are called, like the shepherds, to glorify and praise God, to radiate a Christmas joy to our friends and family and neighbors. You might exchange presents on Christmas morning, and these manger munchies can be your gift to your family. This delicious recipe is a crowd favorite, so make enough to nibble on for Christmas Day and some extra to send home in little goody bags for all your Christmas visitors.

The Nativity
CHRISTMAS | DECEMBER 25

● ◌ ◌ EASY

SERVES: 8

PREPARATION:
10 minutes

INGREDIENTS:
3 cups marshmallows
1 box Rice Chex cereal
3 cups pretzels
1 stick salted butter
¾ cup peanut butter
12 ounces chocolate chips
1 teaspoon vanilla extract
6 cups powdered sugar
Red and green sprinkles

SUPPLIES:
Large bowl for mixing

1. Add the marshmallows, cereal, and pretzels to a large bowl.

2. Chop butter into 1-inch pieces and set aside.

3. Place a saucepan over medium heat and add the butter, stirring until mostly melted.*

4. Add the peanut butter and chocolate chips, stirring continuously until smooth.

5. Turn off the heat and stir in the vanilla extract.

6. Pour the chocolate mixture over the dry ingredients, and stir until coated.

7. Sprinkle the powdered sugar over the mixture, stirring occasionally to coat everything evenly. Add the sprinkles for color, and enjoy!

* You can also melt and combine these ingredients in the microwave. Heat in 30-second increments, stirring thoroughly between.

*In that region there were shepherds living in the fields, keeping
watch over their flock by night. Then an angel of the Lord
stood before them, and the glory of the Lord shone around
them, and they were terrified. But the angel said to them,
"Do not be afraid; for see—I am bringing you good news of
great joy for all the people: to you is born this day in the city
of David a Savior, who is the Messiah, the Lord. This will be
a sign for you: you will find a child wrapped in bands of cloth
and lying in a manger." And suddenly there was with the angel
a multitude of the heavenly host, praising God and saying,*

> *"Glory to God in the highest heaven,
>   and on earth peace among those whom he favors!"*

*When the angels had left them and gone into heaven, the
shepherds said to one another, "Let us go now to Bethlehem and
see this thing that has taken place, which the Lord has made
known to us." So they went with haste and found Mary and
Joseph, and the child lying in the manger. When they saw this,
they made known what had been told them about this child;
and all who heard it were amazed at what the shepherds told
them. But Mary treasured all these words and pondered them
in her heart. The shepherds returned, glorifying and praising
God for all they had heard and seen, as it had been told them.*

—LUKE 2:8–20

ARTWORK
Sandro Botticelli
Mystic Nativity
1500

Yuletide Garland

Red is the color of martyrdom and white is the color of sanctity, so it's fitting to create something red and white to honor St. Stephen, the first martyr. You can make this festive garland to decorate your Christmas tree, the mantle above your fireplace, or other spots around your home. If you are making your garland for your family's Christmas tree, consider making several short garlands rather than one long one. If the garland is long, it's easy to get it all tangled up.

Note: This is for decoration only. The cranberries are raw and tart, and after a few days on the tree, the popcorn will get stale!

St. Stephen

CHRISTMAS | DECEMBER 26

 MODERATE

INGREDIENTS:

Fresh cranberries
(not dried or frozen)

Popcorn
(already popped, not buttered)

SUPPLIES:

Sewing needle

Sturdy thread

1. Ask for a grown-up's assistance to thread your needle and tie a knot at the beginning of your thread so that your popcorn and cranberries don't fall off the end.

2. Alternate popcorn and cranberries to make a lovely design.

3. To complete your garland, tie a knot at the end of your thread.

4. Hang up your garland to bring color and Christmas joy to your home!

But filled with the Holy Spirit, [Stephen] gazed into heaven and saw the glory of God and Jesus standing at the right hand of God. "Look," he said, "I see the heavens opened and the Son of Man standing at the right hand of God!"

ACTS 7:55–56

ARTWORK
Michael Damaskinos
Stoning of Saint Stephen
1591

St. Macarius' Sparkling Sugar Plums

St. Macarius

CHRISTMAS | JANUARY 2

 **EASY**

MAKES:
16 pieces

PREPARATION:
20 minutes

INGREDIENTS:
½ cup chopped walnuts
½ cup almond meal/flour
½ cup pitted dried dates, chopped
¼ cup dried cranberries
½ cup chopped prunes
2 tablespoons cherry preserves/jam
½ teaspoon ground cinnamon
⅛ teaspoon ground cardamom
⅛ teaspoon ground cloves
½ cup sugar

SUPPLIES:
Food processor
(will need adult supervision!)

St. Macarius of Alexandria was a very holy man and wanted to sacrifice all he could for God. Living as a monk in the desert, he would go to the extremes of asceticism (a word we use to describe intense levels of self-discipline) and offer up all of his pain to God. For three years he lived on only one piece of bread a day! You might be surprised to hear that before St. Macarius lived a life of radical simplicity, he was a confectioner. That means that it was young St. Macarius' job to bake and sell sweet pastries and candies all through town. Imagine living around all those sweet treats every day, and being able to eat as many candies and pastries as you would like! Now imagine giving all of that up as an offering to God. Near the end of this Christmas season, let us think about the life of St. Macarius and about little sacrifices we could make to show our love for others and for God.

"The children were nestled all snug in their beds, While visions of sugar-plums danced in their heads." A sugar plum can be the perfect sweet treat in the Christmas season. Nutty and gooey and coated in sugar, these goodies can also remind us of the confectioner-turned-monk, St. Macarius.

1. Preheat the oven to 350°F.

2. While it's preheating, spread your chopped walnuts on one half of a baking sheet. On the other half, put the almond flour. When the oven reaches the right temperature, put the baking sheet in the oven for 5 minutes (keep an eye on the nuts and almond flour to make sure they do not burn or get too brown), then remove and let cool.

3. With adult supervision, add dried fruit and toasted walnuts to the food processor and blend until the fruit and nuts are in tiny pieces and starting to stick together.

4. Add the cherry jam, the almond flour, and the spices and pulse until combined.

5. Have an adult remove the mixture from the food processor. Roll the mixture into 1-inch balls. Roll each ball in sugar and serve!

King Cake

Epiphany
CHRISTMAS

 DIFFICULT

SERVES: 8

PREPARATION:

3 hours

CAKE INGREDIENTS:

3½ cups all-purpose flour

2¼ tablespoons yeast

1 cup milk

¼ cup sugar

1 teaspoon salt

2 eggs

6 tablespoons butter
(cut into 12 pieces, then softened)

CINNAMON FILLING:

⅔ cup brown sugar

1½ teaspoons cinnamon

4 tablespoons butter, melted

CREAM CHEESE ICING:

4 ounces softened cream cheese

4 tablespoons softened butter

¾ cup powdered sugar

Optional: green, purple, and yellow/
gold sprinkles / colored sugar

SUPPLIES:

Stand mixer

Baking tray

Rolling pin

Parchment paper

Pizza cutter or sharp knife

Cooking thermometer

The Sunday after January 1st is the Feast of the Epiphany. This feast celebrates the visit of the three kings or magi (wise men). Tradition calls them Caspar, Melchior, and Balthasar. The three kings visited the Holy Family to honor and bring gifts to baby Jesus. On this day we remember these holy men who followed the star from far away in the East and showed us that Jesus is the Savior of the whole world.

In New Orleans, Epiphany is the beginning of "Carnival," which is celebrated by baking King Cakes (named after the three kings). Bakeries make delicious glazed and decorated cakes to honor the magi. This recipe is a little tricky and takes about 3 hours to make, so you may need the help of a grown-up to complete it. But the end result is worth it!

1. Combine 2½ cups of the flour with the yeast in a mixing bowl. Use the paddle attachment of the stand mixer.

2. Add the milk, sugar, and salt to a saucepan. Cook this mixture over medium heat. You'll want to dissolve the sugar and the salt and have the mixture reach 120°F.

3. Add the contents of the saucepan to the mixing bowl and use the paddle attachment on low to mix the dough. Add the first egg and wait for it to be mixed with the dough and then add the second egg.

4. Switch to the dough hook attachment. Add ½ cup of flour and mix until combined, then add the last ½ cup of flour. Keep mixing until all the flour is combined with the dough. Add the pieces of softened butter one at a time and let the butter combine with the dough before adding another.

5. Knead the dough for 1 minute on a lightly floured surface and roll into a ball. Let the ball of dough rest in a greased bowl with plastic wrap in your refrigerator for 1 hour.

6. While the dough is in the fridge, add the sugar, cinnamon, and melted butter to a small bowl and combine.

7. After 1 hour of chilling, bring out the dough and roll it into a large rectangle on a lightly floured surface.

8. Add the cinnamon filling to half of the rectangle (longways), then fold the dough over the cinnamon filling side and pinch the edges together to keep the cinnamon filling from leaking out.

9. Use a pizza cutter or sharp knife to cut the dough into 3 long pieces. Pinch these 3 pieces at the top and then braid them together. Pinch the end of the 3 strands of dough together.

King Cake (Continued)

10. Pull the ends to stretch out your braided dough and then connect the ends together to make a circle and place on a cooking sheet with parchment paper. Cover with plastic wrap and let the dough rise for 1 hour.

11. Preheat the oven to 350°F. Take off the plastic wrap and add your king cake on the cookie sheet to the oven.

12. Bake the cake until golden brown (about 30 minutes). Let it cool while you make the cream cheese icing. (If you ice the cake when it's warm, the icing will melt and drip off your cake.)

13. Add the cream cheese and butter to the mixing bowl and mix until smooth. Add the powdered sugar and mix until combined. Once the king cake is completely cooled, decorate with your cream cheese icing on top and then add purple, green, and yellow/gold sprinkles or colored sugar.

When they saw that the star had stopped, they were overwhelmed with joy. On entering the house, they saw the child with Mary his mother; and they knelt down and paid him homage. Then, opening their treasure chests, they offered him gifts of gold, frankincense, and myrrh. And having been warned in a dream not to return to Herod, they left for their own country by another road.

—MATTHEW 2:10–12

ARTWORK
Gentile da Fabriano
Adoration of the Magi
1423

Ordinary Time

Be Thou my Vision, O Lord of my heart;

Naught be all else to me, save that Thou art.

Thou my best Thought, by day or by night,

Waking or sleeping, Thy presence my light.

A Time to Grow

Ordinary Time is the liturgical season between the Christmas season and Lent and between Pentecost and Advent. It is a time for us to live out our Catholic faith and grow in virtue. And what better example of virtue and faith than the saints? Ordinary Time is a great season to learn about, befriend, and imitate the Church's great saints.

During Ordinary Time between Epiphany and the beginning of the season of Lent on Ash Wednesday, we can celebrate saints whose feast days fall during this time, including St. Brigid of Kildare and St. Paul Miki.

St. Brigid's Endless Herbed Butter

St. Brigid

ORDINARY TIME | FEBRUARY 1

 ● ◐ ◌ EASY

St. Brigid of Kildare was an Irish saint who was friends with St. Patrick, the saint who helped share the Gospel with the Irish people. Her mother was enslaved by a pagan chieftain, and Brigid worked as a shepherdess and was known for her generous heart. When she would churn butter, she would give as much as she could to the poor, but her butter dish would miraculously never go empty! When Brigid was old enough to be married, she decided that she was called to give her life to God in a different way. This angered many men who found her beautiful and wanted to marry her. To solve this problem, she prayed to God that he would take away her beauty, and he did—but only until her suitors left. St. Brigid helped to form the first convent of Ireland, offering a place for both priests and nuns to live, study, and pray.

To remember the story of St. Brigid's butter, make this simple herbed butter to enjoy with good common bread (page 100). If you don't have fresh herbs, you can use dried ones (but just decrease the amount by half if you use dried).

YIELDS:
1 pound of butter

PREPARATION:
15 minutes

INGREDIENTS:
1 quart heavy whipping cream
2 garlic cloves, minced
1 tablespoon fresh thyme
¼ teaspoon black pepper
1 tablespoon fresh oregano
½ tablespoon fresh rosemary
Salt to taste

SUPPLIES:
Large mason jar

1. Place your heavy whipping cream in the mason jar.

2. Shake the jar for 12 to 14 minutes. About 10 minutes in, you'll have whipped cream, but keep going until you can feel lumps rattling around in the jar.

3. Once the liquid has fully separated from the solids, take out the lumps of butter and place them on a paper towel or cheese cloth. Squeeze out all the additional liquid and form a ball of butter.

4. Run under cold water to fully clear off all the additional liquid or fat.

5. Add the herbs, garlic, salt, and pepper to your butter and serve.

Miki's Maki

St. Paul Miki

ORDINARY TIME (OR LENT) | FEBRUARY 6

● ● ◦ MODERATE

Born into a wealthy family in Japan, St. Paul Miki joined a religious order called the Society of Jesus (or the Jesuits). God gave St. Paul Miki a talent for preaching, and he became well-known for his powerful sermons. At this time, Christians in Japan were being persecuted. St. Paul Miki was arrested and forced to march six hundred miles to Nagasaki to stand trial. While this journey must have been full of suffering, St. Paul Miki and his fellow prisoners spent their days singing hymns to God as they marched. He was martyred in 1597, but before he was crucified, he preached one last sermon, forgiving his executioners and encouraging others to follow Christ.

Sushi became popular in Japan hundreds of years ago. Why not honor St. Paul Miki and his holy companions by making this recipe for maki (a kind of sushi) with your family? You can choose which ingredients you'd like to include and create rolls with different combinations. This recipe is very simple to make, but you will need some special supplies like nori (dried seaweed sheets), sushi rice, and a sushi mat.

SERVES: 4

PREPARATION:
45 minutes

INGREDIENTS:
2 cups sushi rice
2 cups water
3 tablespoons rice vinegar
1½ tablespoon sugar
Pinch of salt
1 package of nori sheets (dried seaweed)
Soy sauce

FILLING OPTIONS:
Chopped cucumber, avocado, lettuce, carrots, green onions, or cilantro.
Cream cheese or spicy mayo (mayonnaise and sriracha).

SUPPLIES:
Saucepan for cooking rice
Sushi mat

1. Rinse the rice in cool water and drain. Repeat 2 more times.

2. Bring the rice and water to a boil. Reduce to simmer and cover. Cook for 16 minutes or until water is absorbed. Remove from heat but keep covered for 5 minutes.

3. Mix vinegar, sugar, and salt in a bowl. Pour mixture into the rice (after cooking). Stir the rice to mix everything evenly. Before the rice is ready for you to handle, it will need to cool. While the sushi rice cools (about 15 minutes), prepare your fillings.

4. Lay out 1 nori sheet on the sushi mat. The nori has a rough side and a smooth side. The rough side should be facing up.

5. Wet your hands (it helps to have a cup of water handy) and take 1 handful of the cooled sushi rice. Place the rice in the middle of the nori sheet and spread to the sides in a thin layer. If the rice is sticking too much to your fingers, wet them in the water again. Cover all of the nori except for 1 inch at the top. The rice should be about 1/4 inch thick.

6. Lay your fillings out on the rice. (Don't overfill.)

7. Starting at the bottom, slowly roll the sushi up toward the top. This is where the sushi mat really comes in handy. Once the sushi is rolled up, the top of the nori sheet without rice should wrap around and form a seal. You can add a little bit of water to get the end of the nori to stick and seal.

8. Have a grown-up cut the roll with a very sharp knife into 8 pieces. Serve with soy sauce.

"The only reason for my being killed is that I have taught the doctrine of Christ. I certainly did teach the doctrine of Christ. I thank God it is for this reason I die. I believe that I am telling only the truth before I die. I know you believe me and I want to say to you all once again: Ask Christ to help you to become happy. I obey Christ. After Christ's example I forgive my persecutors. I do not hate them. I ask God to have pity on all, and I hope my blood will fall on my fellow men as a fruitful rain."

—ST. PAUL MIKI'S WORDS FROM THE CROSS

ARTWORK
Unknown
Martyrdom of Nagasaki
1622

Lent

O sacred Head, now wounded,

with grief and shame weighed down,

now scornfully surrounded

with thorns, thine only crown;

O sacred Head, what glory,

what bliss till now was thine!

Yet, though despised and gory,

I joy to call thee mine.

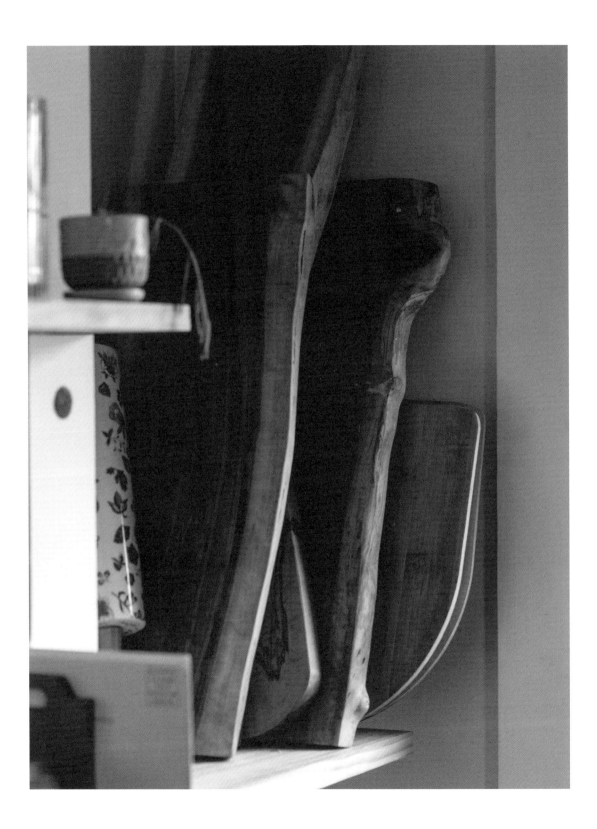

Prepare Your Hearts

There are many days of feasting and celebration in the Church's calendar, but Lent is not one of these festive times. Lent is a time of preparation. We are preparing to walk with Jesus to his Crucifixion. And we remember how Jesus died for our sins in order to save us.

During the season of Lent, we focus on penitence. We think about ways that we have sinned and how our sins grieve God. We show him that we are sorry for our sins and we consider ways that he wants us to grow in holiness.

The Church offers us tried and true ways of participating in this season of preparation and penitence: fasting, prayer, and almsgiving. Fasting is the practice of saying "no" to something we want, such as favorite snacks, TV shows, or video games. Fasting helps strengthen us spiritually so that we can say yes to God, even when it's difficult. It is common to give up a certain food that we like during Lent. St. Basil the Great says, "The more you deny the flesh, the more you render the soul radiant with spiritual health." Fasting helps us to become more spiritually healthy.

Focusing on good habits of prayer is another key Lenten practice. We might pray a daily Rosary or make time for the Stations of the Cross and other beautiful prayers of the Church that help us meditate on Jesus' sacrifice for us. The third practice of Lent, almsgiving, is the practice of giving to those who are in need. Whether donating money to a charity, helping to stock a local food pantry, or providing diapers or baby formula for mothers in crisis, there are many ways to give alms. Talk to your family and consider how you can participate in the Lenten season together.

Shrovetide Pancakes

Shrove Tuesday
ORDINARY TIME

● ● ○ MODERATE

Lent is a time for us to sacrifice little things to bring us closer to Jesus. We can consider what to give up that would help us become more holy and offer that sacrifice to God. A long time ago, it was common practice during Lent to give up many foods as a Lenten practice of penitence. People in Britain would give up the eggs and butter in their cupboards, so the day before Ash Wednesday would be the perfect time to use up all of those ingredients so they didn't go bad during the long weeks of Lent. They called this day Shrove Tuesday because Lent was a time to be "shriven" or cleansed of sin. What better way to use up eggs and butter than to make pancakes!

SERVES: 6

PREPARATION:
25 minutes

INGREDIENTS:
2 cups flour
2 teaspoons baking powder
¼ teaspoon salt
2 eggs (beaten)
2 cups milk
2 tablespoons melted butter
(Oil for griddle)

SUPPLIES:
Griddle or pan
Spatula to flip pancakes

1. Combine flour, baking powder, and salt in a bowl. Add eggs, milk, and melted butter and whisk together.

2. Heat a little bit of oil in the pan or griddle over medium heat.

3. Spoon batter for 3–4 pancakes onto pan. Cook on the first side until little bubbles form, then flip and cook for another two minutes on the second side.

4. Top with any of the following: maple syrup, fruit, whipped cream, chocolate chips, powdered sugar.

Ash Wednesday Common Bread

Ash Wednesday

LENT

● ● ○ MODERATE

SERVES: 4–5

PREPARATION:

1 hour

INGREDIENTS:

4¼ cups all-purpose flour

3 teaspoons instant yeast

2 teaspoons kosher salt

2¼ cups warm water

SUPPLIES:

Dutch oven

Large mixing bowl

Tea towel or cloth

Parchment paper

On Ash Wednesday, the Church around the world starts to observe Lent with Masses and fasting. When we go to Mass on Ash Wednesday, the priest will mark the sign of the cross in ashes on our foreheads. This is a sign of sorrow for our sins and a reminder of our mortality.

On this somber day, Catholics over the age of fourteen are called to fast (only eat one simple meal and two small snacks) and "abstain" (avoid eating meat for the whole day). To prepare for a meatless dinner on Ash Wednesday, making bread during the day can be a task that helps us think about the purpose of Lent.

As Catholics, bread is probably the food we think about the most. In the Bible, we see it in the Old Testament as manna (bread from heaven that fed the Israelites in the wilderness), and in the New Testament, Jesus tells us that he is the bread of life. Every day around the world, priests celebrate the Holy Sacrifice of the Mass, where God turns bread into the very Body of Christ. We should spend each day of Lent calling to mind the sacrifice of Jesus on the cross, and sacrificing our little luxuries in the name of Jesus, in preparation for Easter.

This bread recipe is great for a grilled cheese sandwich and to pair with a good meatless soup.

1. Mix the dry ingredients in a large bowl. Keep the yeast and salt to either side of the bowl before mixing in order to preserve the strength of the yeast.

2. Slowly add the water and mix, mix, mix!

3. Once the dough has become a sticky ball with no lumps of flour, cover the bowl with a damp tea towel and place in a warm spot for rising. (An oven—turned off—with the oven light on is a great spot.)

4. Allow the bread to rise for 2 hours, then remove the dough and preheat the oven to 450°F, with your Dutch oven and lid inside.

5. While your oven is preheating, stick your fingers under the bottom of the dough and start pulling sections over and around to the top, until every section comes together in the center and it forms a ball or boule.

6. Pick your boule up out of the bowl and flip upside down and place on a piece of parchment paper. Dust your hands with flour, then cup your hands and smooth the boule from top to bottom. Do this until the top of the boule looks smooth.

Ash Wednesday Common Bread (Continued)

7. Dust the top with flour and score your bread along the top, making sure to cut at least 1/2-inch-deep.

8. Ask a grown-up to open the oven and carefully take the hot lid off of the Dutch oven, then transfer the parchment paper and boule into the Dutch oven. Replace the lid.

9. Bake for 30 minutes, then have a grown-up remove the lid. Bake for an additional 15 minutes until golden brown.*

10. Remove the bread from the Dutch oven and allow to fully cool before slicing. Serve with St. Brigid's endless herbed butter!

Oven times might vary, so if you have a thermometer, the inside of the bread should be at 190°F.

Zeppole di San Giuseppe

St. Joseph

LENT | MARCH 19

● ● ○ MODERATE

In the midst of the quiet and penitential Lenten months, our dear St. Joseph offers us all a little light! St. Joseph is such a beloved figure in our faith. As the foster father of Jesus and husband of the Blessed Virgin Mary, Joseph inspires a humble devotion to living our lives in the service of God. Because of St. Joseph's important role in the Holy Family, the Church names his feast day as a *solemnity*, a feast day of the highest kind. St. Joseph's feast day occurs in the middle of Lent, and Catholics around the world celebrate this saint.

Legend has it that in the Middle Ages, Sicily was suffering from a famine: because of a lengthy drought, there was very little food for the people, and many died. The Sicilians prayed to St. Joseph, begging him to ask God for rain and for the famine to end. In return, they promised to carry on his legacy and to celebrate his feast day with St. Joseph's Tables: family altars in the homes decorated with candles, religious objects, and sweet foods. St. Joseph delivered on the promise: rain came, and the Sicilians were delivered from the famine. Today, families still prepare St. Joseph's Tables at home, decorating them with candles, sweet-smelling flowers, and, of course, delectable treats like *zeppole*.

Zeppole are crispy little donuts fried and coated in powdered sugar—sweet on the outside and fluffy on the inside. The secret to the melt-in-your-mouth interior is the ricotta cheese. (So make sure you don't forget it!) *Zeppole* are best served warm, paired with hot chocolate!

SERVES: 6–10

PREPARATION:
30 minutes

INGREDIENTS:
2 eggs
1 cup all-purpose flour
2¼ teaspoons baking powder
Pinch of salt
2 teaspoons vanilla extract
¼ cup white sugar
1 cup ricotta cheese
Coconut oil
Powdered sugar (or cinnamon sugar)

SUPPLIES:
Large mixing bowl
Spatula
Pot
Cookie scoop
Cooking thermometer

1. In a large mixing bowl, beat eggs with a whisk until frothy.

2. Stir in your flour, baking powder, salt, vanilla extract, and sugar until just combined. Make sure not to overmix.

3. Using a spatula, fold in your ricotta. Don't stir! Just fold your dough on top of the ricotta until it mixes in evenly.

4. Heat 2 inches of oil in a pot to 375°F.

5. Using a cookie scoop, drop the batter into hot oil. (Spray with cooking spray in advance for best results.).

6. Cook for 3 to 4 minutes, turning frequently until golden brown, then set on paper towels to drain.

7. Immediately dust with powdered sugar or cinnamon sugar and enjoy!

*"Go to Joseph! Have recourse with special
confidence to St. Joseph, for his protection
is most powerful, as he is the patron of the
universal Church."*

—BLESSED POPE PIUS IX

ARTWORK
Guido Reni
St. Joseph with Infant Christ in His Arms
1620s

Gabriel's Wings Alfredo

The Annunciation
LENT | MARCH 25

● ● ○ MODERATE

SERVES: 4

PREPARATION:
25 minutes

INGREDIENTS:
2 cups farfalle pasta
2 tablespoons olive oil
2 tablespoons minced garlic
1 medium onion, diced
1 teaspoon salt
1 teaspoon dried rosemary
1 teaspoon dried oregano
¾ cup butter
1½ cup heavy whipping cream
2 cups parmesan cheese
1 teaspoon black pepper

SUPPLIES:
Pot for boiling pasta
Saucepan
Skillet
Cheese grater for parmesan

"Hail, full of grace, the Lord is with thee."

These are the striking words the angel Gabriel spoke to Our Lady before she said yes to being the mother of Jesus. There is no other saint closer to Jesus than Our Lady. As Catholics, we see the Annunciation as the beginning of Jesus' earthly time, and we recognize the holiness of his mother Mary in that moment. Her *fiat*, her yes to God, should be our model whenever we are asked to be holy in a way that seems impossible. The Annunciation is the perfect day to consider, "Where did Jesus ask me to say yes today? Did I do so joyfully? Did he ask me to be patient with my siblings? To obey my parents? To do my homework well?" On today's feast, find little ways to say yes to God.

The Annunciation recognizes the beginning of the Holy Family, and this feast is a beautiful way to come together and share a meal with *your* family. Try praying the Angelus, a traditional Catholic prayer that helps us reflect on the Annunciation.

You can also try making this delicious pasta dish. If you can, make the sauce over farfalle pasta. (Farfalle is Italian for "butterfly wings," but we think it looks like angel wings—like Gabriel's!)

1. Heat water in a pot for your pasta and then cook the pasta according to its instructions. While the pasta is cooking, make your alfredo sauce.

2. Add the olive oil to a saucepan over medium heat and heat for 2 minutes.

3. Add your onion and garlic to the pan and sauté for 5 minutes.

4. Add the seasonings and stir.

5. In a large skillet, heat the butter and cream over low heat. Stir constantly and slowly as it cooks until the cream mixture is hot and lightly simmers for at least 2 minutes.

6. Add the contents of the saucepan with the seasonings, garlic, and onion to the cream mixture.

7. Once mixed, add in your parmesan cheese and stir.

8. Serve your sauce over pasta and add your black pepper for a final touch!

℣. *The Angel of the Lord declared to Mary:*
℟. *And she conceived of the Holy Spirit.*

Hail Mary, full of grace, the Lord is with thee; blessed art thou among women and blessed is the fruit of thy womb, Jesus. Holy Mary, Mother of God, pray for us sinners, now and at the hour of our death. Amen.

℣. *Behold the handmaid of the Lord:*
℟. *Be it done unto me according to Thy word.*

Hail Mary...

℣. *And the Word was made Flesh:*
℟. *And dwelt among us.*

Hail Mary...

℣. *Pray for us, O Holy Mother of God,*
℟. *that we may be made worthy of the promises of Christ.*

Let us pray:

Pour forth, we beseech Thee, O Lord, Thy grace into our hearts; that we, to whom the Incarnation of Christ, Thy Son, was made known by the message of an angel, may by His Passion and Cross be brought to the glory of His Resurrection, through the same Christ Our Lord.

Amen.

ARTWORK
Sandro Botticelli
Annunciation
c. 1490–1495

Holy Week

Holy Week is observed from Palm Sunday to Easter Sunday, and it is the most important week in the Christian Year. This week invites us to journey with Jesus and Mary through the days leading up to the Crucifixion and the Resurrection. The liturgies and traditions of Holy Week help us to walk through the events in the Gospel story and participate in this sacred time.

Important Events of Holy Week:

PALM SUNDAY: Jesus rides a donkey into Jerusalem.

SPY WEDNESDAY: Judas betrays Jesus for thirty pieces of silver.

HOLY THURSDAY: Jesus and the disciples gather for the Last Supper, where Jesus washes their feet and institutes the Eucharist. Afterward, Jesus prays in the Garden of Gethsemane, is betrayed by Judas, and is arrested.

GOOD FRIDAY: Jesus is condemned to execution by Pontius Pilate. He is whipped, stripped of his clothes, and mocked with a crown of thorns. He carries the cross on his journey to Golgotha, the place of crucifixion, and is killed.

HOLY SATURDAY: Jesus' body rests in a tomb provided by Joseph of Arimathea.

EASTER SUNDAY: Jesus is raised from the dead!

Good Friday Potato and Leek Soup

Good Friday is one of the most important days in our liturgical year. We come together as a Church, as one family, to memorialize the sacrifice that Jesus underwent for our sins. On Good Friday, Catholics are called to fast and abstain from meat. This makes cooking on Good Friday a little difficult! Luckily, this potato and leek soup is perfect for Good Friday dinner—especially paired with our Ash Wednesday Common Bread (recipe on page 100).

Good Friday
LENT

 **MODERATE**

SERVES: 8

PREPARATION:
1 hour

INGREDIENTS:
4-5 leeks, cleaned and sliced
3 tablespoons butter
6 cloves of garlic
1 tablespoon fresh thyme
2 pounds yukon gold potatoes, thinly sliced
4 cups vegetable broth
1 teaspoon salt
½ cup heavy cream
Pepper, to taste
Grated parmesan cheese
2 tablespoons chopped chives

SUPPLIES:
Dutch oven or large soup pot
Optional: immersion blender

1. Peel back and wash the leeks. Slice leeks into ¼-inch slices.

2. Heat butter in a large dutch oven on your stove over medium heat. Sauté leeks, garlic, and thyme until fragrant and wilted (approximately 10 minutes).

3. Add the potatoes, vegetable broth, and salt. Bring to a boil, then reduce heat to a low simmer (covered) for 25 minutes. Stir occasionally.

4. Ask a grown-up to use an immersion blender to blend the soup. If you don't have an immersion blender, you can let the soup cool and transfer it to a regular blender to mix. You might have to do this in sections, until the entire soup has been blended.

5. Add the heavy cream and salt and pepper to taste. If you used an immersion blender and the soup is still hot, make sure to mix the heavy cream well so as not to curdle the cream. If you used a regular blender, add the cream, reheat the soup to serving temperature, and then add the salt and pepper.

6. Serve with grated parmesan cheese and chives.

Eternal Father, I offer you the Body and Blood,
Soul and Divinity of your dearly beloved Son, our
Lord, Jesus Christ, in atonement for our sins and
those of the whole world.

—FROM THE CHAPLET OF DIVINE MERCY

Hot Cross Buns

Holy Saturday

LENT

● ● ○ MODERATE

After Good Friday, there is one more day before we celebrate the glory of Jesus' Resurrection. This day is Holy Saturday—a day when we observe the great silence of the grieving world when Jesus was dead in the tomb. The disciples were sad and afraid, unsure of what would happen. But we know that this day of grief is overturned by the joy of Easter!

On Holy Saturday, we make our final preparations for Easter—whether we're attending the Easter Vigil Mass on Saturday night or Mass on Easter morning. We might help our families tidy up the house or start preparing the food for the Easter Sunday feast. We might dye eggs or do other quiet tasks while thinking about God's sacrifice for us.

In some parts of the world, simple sweet rolls are a traditional Holy Week snack. As you get ready for Easter on Holy Saturday, you can spend part of your day preparing these buns, marked with a cross to represent the Crucifixion.

SERVES: 6

PREPARATION:
30 minutes

INGREDIENTS:
2 cups self-rising flour
1½ teaspoons cinnamon
¼ teaspoon nutmeg
¼ teaspoon ground cloves
4 tablespoons brown sugar
1½ cups Greek yogurt
2 teaspoons vanilla extract

ICING FOR CROSS:
½ cup powdered sugar
Splash of milk

SUPPLIES:
Baking sheet
Parchment paper
Small bowl for mixing icing
Piping bag (or plastic bag with a corner cut)

1. Preheat oven to 390°F.

2. Line a baking sheet with parchment paper.

3. Add flour, cinnamon, nutmeg, cloves, and brown sugar to a bowl and whisk.

4. Add yogurt and vanilla extract and mix. You can start with a spoon, but you will have to use your hands to work the dough.

5. On a lightly floured surface (to prevent sticking), begin to knead the dough (pushing it down with your hands, folding it over, and pushing it again). You can stop once it forms a ball.

6. Divide the dough into 6 balls and set on parchment paper.

7. Place the baking tray into the oven for 20 minutes.

8. Make your icing by mixing the powdered sugar with a splash of milk. If it's too dry, add another splash of milk. But you'll want it to be nice and thick so it keeps its shape when you pipe it.

9. After the buns cool, pipe a cross with your icing.

Easter

Jesus Christ is risen today (Alleluia!)

Our triumphant holy day (Alleluia!)

Who did once upon the cross (Alleluia!)

Suffer to redeem our loss (Alleluia!).

Hymns of praise then let us sing (Alleluia!)

Unto Christ, our heavenly King (Alleluia!)

Who endured the cross and grave (Alleluia!)

Sinners to redeem and save (Alleluia!).

But the pains which he endured (Alleluia!)

Our salvation have procured (Alleluia!)

Now above the sky he's king (Alleluia!)

Where the angels ever sing (Alleluia!).

New Life in Christ

Easter Sunday begins fifty days of feasting and celebrating the Resurrection. We rejoice because Jesus was raised from the dead—never to die again!

On this holiest of days, the impossible was made possible. Death itself was conquered by God's sacrificial love.

It's beautiful that during this time of year, God's creation seems to join us in celebrating the Resurrection. Green leaves grow once again on the trees, and flowers open, bringing color and beauty to our eyes. The short, dark days of winter lengthen into spring sunshine. The whole world rejoices that Christ has risen!

During these days of Easter, we bring back the good things we sacrificed during Lent. If you gave up ice cream, for instance, have a scoop! After the long forty days of Lenten preparation, you are probably eager to join the Easter party.

The story of Easter may be so familiar to us that we forget what an unbelievable miracle God performed by raising Jesus from the dead and opening the way of salvation to us all. In other words, Easter Sunday not only celebrates when the stone was rolled away from the tomb and Jesus walked out of the grave. It also celebrates the beginning of our new life in Christ. As the sacrament of Baptism reminds us, we are joined with Christ in his death and his Resurrection. We don't have to fear death anymore, because Christ is victorious over death and invites us to join him in this new Easter life.

Easter Edible Flower Salad

Easter is such an important holy day that families often have special food traditions to celebrate it. Perhaps your family has ham or lamb, deviled eggs, or a fancy dessert you always share together.

This simple but delicious Easter salad can accompany your meal and add some color and beauty. The edible flowers are a fun touch, reminding us of the vibrant new life that we are called to in Christ! (But be sure only to use flowers like nasturtiums that are safe to eat.)

Easter Sunday

EASTER

● ◌ ◌ **EASY**

SERVES: 6

PREPARATION:

5 minutes

INGREDIENTS:

¼ cup pistachios

2 cups mixed berries (blueberries, strawberries, and raspberries)

¼ cup goat cheese

4 cups spring mix

2 cups baby spinach

Edible flowers (like nasturtiums)

DRESSING:

1 tablespoon balsamic vinegar

3 tablespoons olive oil

1 teaspoon poppyseeds

1 teaspoon Dijon mustard

1 teaspoon honey

Salt

Pepper

SUPPLIES:

Large bowl

Mason jar

1. Shell the pistachios and wash the fruit.

2. Cut the greens off the strawberries and cut the strawberries into slivers. Then crumble the goat cheese.

3. Add your spring mix and spinach to a large bowl, then add the other ingredients. For decoration, add edible fresh flowers, like nasturtiums, or edible dried flowers, like globe amaranth, red globe amaranth, or chrysanthemum.

4. In a mason jar, combine all the ingredients for the dressing and shake it up. Dress the salad, and it's ready to enjoy!

Early on the first day of the week, while it was still dark, Mary Magdalene came to the tomb and saw that the stone had been removed from the tomb. So she ran and went to Simon Peter and the other disciple, the one whom Jesus loved, and said to them, "They have taken the Lord out of the tomb, and we do not know where they have laid him." Then Peter and the other disciple set out and went toward the tomb. The two were running together, but the other disciple outran Peter and reached the tomb first. He bent down to look in and saw the linen wrappings lying there, but he did not go in. Then Simon Peter came, following him, and went into the tomb. He saw the linen wrappings lying there, and the cloth that had been on Jesus' head, not lying with the linen wrappings but rolled up in a place by itself. Then the other disciple, who reached the tomb first, also went in, and he saw and believed; for as yet they did not understand the scripture, that he must rise from the dead.

—JOHN 20:1–9

ARTWORK
Andrea Mantegna
The Resurrection
1457–1459

St. George's Dragon Eggs

St. George was a brave Roman soldier and devout Christian. When the emperor Diocletian began persecuting Christians, St. George left his position in the emperor's army. As a result, the authorities tortured and beheaded him. Sacred art featuring St. George often depicts him slaying a dragon and rescuing a maiden, as he does in a medieval collection of saint stories called *The Golden Legend*. He is the patron saint of England.

Remember courageous St. George and the fierce dragon he conquered by making these hardboiled eggs decorated with a fun and colorful pattern to look like dragon eggs.

Warning: This recipe uses food coloring, which can get messy. Be sure to use adult supervision.

St. George

EASTER | APRIL 23

 MODERATE

PREPARATION:

1.5 hours

INGREDIENTS:

Eggs
Water
White vinegar
Food coloring
Ice

SUPPLIES:

Plastic freezer bag
Saucepan or pot with lid
Bowl

1. Add eggs to a saucepan or pot and cover them with water.

2. Add a splash of white vinegar to the pot.

3. On the stove, bring the water to a boil over high heat.

4. When your water is boiling with big bubbles, turn off the heat and cover with the lid.

5. Leave the pot on the stovetop for 10 minutes and fill a large bowl with ice and water.

6. After 10 minutes, carefully transfer your eggs with a large spoon into the bowl of ice water and leave them in the ice water for 5 minutes.

7. Use a spoon to lightly tap on the eggs so that cracks form in the shell. (You want cracks all over, but you don't want to break through the shell completely.)

8. Add a splash of food coloring to a large freezer bag, then add your eggs to the bag and gently move them around so that the food coloring can make its way into the cracks. Leave them in the bag for 15 minutes.

9. Place a paper towel on a plate. Take the eggs out of the bag and let them dry on the paper towel.

10. Run the eggs under water and gently peel them to uncover the dragon egg design!

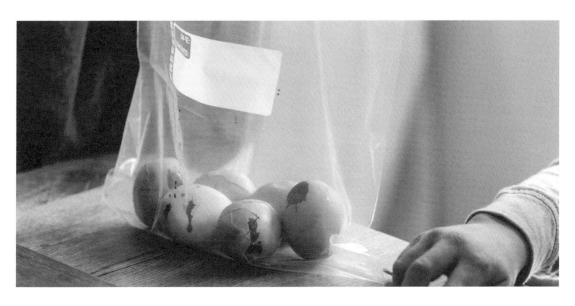

"Doubt not. Believe in God and Jesus Christ, and be baptized, and I shall slay the dragon."

—ST. GEORGE, *THE GOLDEN LEGEND*

St. Catherine's Fiery Tomato Risotto

St. Catherine of Siena said, "If you are what you should be, you will set the whole world on fire!" A young Italian girl in the fourteenth century, St. Catherine loved God with all her heart. She was expected by her family to marry well, but Catherine knew God was calling her to a different kind of life. She was a brilliant theologian and is now honored as a Doctor of the Church. Although she was never taught to read or write, she was miraculously given the gift of literacy, and this unusual Italian girl became an advisor to influential figures, including the pope! Pope St. John Paul II named her one of the six patron saints of Europe.

Risotto is a traditional food in Northern Italy. This is not a difficult recipe, but it does take time and requires using the stovetop.

Note: You must use arborio rice or the texture won't be right.

St. Catherine of Siena

EASTER | APRIL 29

● ● ◉ MODERATE

SERVES: 3

PREPARATION:

1 hour

INGREDIENTS:

1 medium sweet onion, diced

2 tablespoons butter

4 cups chicken broth

1 cup arborio rice

¼ cup sun-dried tomatoes in oil, diced

½ cup grated Pecorino Romano or parmesan cheese

SUPPLIES:

2 saucepans

1. In a saucepan, sauté the onion in butter over medium heat until softened (about 5 minutes). Warm up the broth in a separate saucepan.

2. Stir the arborio rice into the saucepan with onion and butter (saving the broth for later). Toast the rice for a minute or two, stirring continuously.

3. Reduce the heat to low. Add broth to the rice ½ cup at a time and stir. Once the broth is absorbed (it will take a couple of minutes), add another ½ cup and so on until all the broth is absorbed. The risotto should be soft and creamy when it is done.

4. When the rice is almost done, add the sun-dried tomatoes.

5. Once the rice is fully cooked, remove from heat and allow it to cool for a few minutes. Add the cheese and stir. Serve warm!

"We are of such value to God that he came to live among us . . . and to guide us home. He will go to any length to seek us, even to being lifted high upon the cross to draw us back to himself. We can only respond by loving God for his love."

—ST. CATHERINE OF SIENA

ARTWORK
Giovanni di Paolo
*The Miraculous Communion of
Saint Catherine of Siena*
15TH CENTURY

Ascension Clouds

The Feast of the Ascension commemorates Jesus' Ascension into heaven to join God the Father. This feast, celebrated forty days after Easter, reminds us that we, too, are invited to spend eternity in heaven, and that we are tasked with bringing the Gospel to others: to our family, our friends, our classmates, and our neighbors. We're called to be joyful signs of God's love to everyone we meet!

To celebrate this feast day, create your own edible clouds, just like the one that lifted Jesus back up to our heavenly Father.

The Ascension
EASTER

 ● ● ◉ MODERATE

SERVES: 6

PREPARATION:
1.5 hours

INGREDIENTS:
4 egg whites
½ teaspoon vanilla extract
½ teaspoon almond extract
⅛ teaspoon cream of tartar
¾ cup granulated sugar
Sparkle sprinkles for decoration

SUPPLIES:
Stand mixer (like a KitchenAid)
Parchment paper

1. Preheat the oven to 200°F.

2. Add the egg whites, cream of tartar, vanilla extract, and almond extract to a mixer.

3. Beat the mixture on medium until the consistency looks like foam (or clouds).

4. Switch the speed to high and add the sugar.

5. Beat the mixture until you see stiff peaks.

6. Spoon the mixture onto a parchment paper-lined baking sheet, forming the shape of a cloud. Leave 2 inches of space between cookies. (Tip: add small dollops of the mixture to the corners of the parchment paper to keep the paper from rolling up.)

7. Bake for 45 minutes in the oven.

8. Turn off the heat and leave in the oven another 30 minutes.

9. Remove from the oven.

10. Dust with sparkle sprinkles and let your clouds cool before eating.

When he had said this, as they were watching, he was lifted up, and a cloud took him out of their sight.

—ACTS 1:9

ARTWORK
Fra Angelico
The Ascension of Christ, The Last Judgment, Pentecost (Corsini Triptych)
1447–1448

Le Colombier Dove Cake

At Pentecost, the Holy Spirit filled the disciples with the abilities they needed to evangelize, including the ability to speak many languages, even those they had never known before. The Holy Spirit inspires the faithful here on earth in all the ways we need to best preach the Gospel.

Pentecost is the birthday of the Church, and what is a birthday celebration without a cake? In the south of France, the traditional dessert to celebrate Pentecost is *le colombier*—the dove cake! This is a very sweet treat meant to be shared with friends and family.

Pentecost

EASTER

  MODERATE

SERVES: 8

PREPARATION:

1 hour

INGREDIENTS:

¾ cup sour cream

1½ cups granulated sugar

1 egg white and 3 eggs

1½ cups all-purpose flour

¾ cup almond flour
(not almond meal)

3 teaspoons baking powder

¾ teaspoon salt

1 teaspoon almond extract

2 teaspoons vanilla extract

¾ cup melted butter

Fresh strawberries

Fresh blueberries

Fresh blackberries

1 cup almond slices

GLAZE:

2 cups powdered sugar

3 tablespoons milk

1 teaspoon vanilla extract

SUPPLIES:

9-inch spring pan

Bowl for mixing

Whisk

1. Preheat the oven to 350°F.

2. Prepare a 9-inch spring pan with parchment paper. Lightly grease the sides of the pan with butter and set aside.

3. In a bowl, combine the sour cream, sugar, and eggs, whisking until well-blended, making sure to break up the lumps of sour cream.

4. Add the flour, almond flour, baking powder, salt, and extracts to the liquid mixture, whisking until smooth.

5. Melt the butter and mix into the batter.

6. Pour the mixture into the spring pan and bake for 40 minutes.

7. Test for readiness with a toothpick in the center. If it comes out clean, the cake is ready.

8. Cool the cake for 10 minutes.

9. While cooling, mix the glaze ingredients together in a separate bowl, adding milk until the consistency is smooth and liquid-like.

10. While the cake is still warm, brush the glaze over the top of the cake, layering the glaze until it's used up.

11. For added decoration, add almond slices to the top in a pattern and dust with a layer of powdered sugar! Serve with fresh fruit.

When the day of Pentecost had come, they were all together in one place. And suddenly from heaven there came a sound like the rush of a violent wind, and it filled the entire house where they were sitting. Divided tongues, as of fire, appeared among them, and a tongue rested on each of them. All of them were filled with the Holy Spirit and began to speak in other languages, as the Spirit gave them ability.

—ACTS 2:1–4

ARTWORK
Juan Bautista Maíno
Pentecost
1615–1620

Ordinary Time

Come, thou Fount of every blessing;

tune my heart to sing thy grace;

streams of mercy, never ceasing,

call for songs of loudest praise.

Teach me some melodious sonnet,

sung by flaming tongues above;

praise the mount! I'm fixed upon it,

mount of God's unchanging love!

More Time to Grow

The longest stretch of Ordinary Time occurs between Pentecost and the season of Advent when the liturgical year starts over again. Saints we celebrate during this time include St. John the Baptist, Bl. Pier Giorgio Frassati, St. Charbel Makhlouf, St. Hildegard of Bingen, St. Michael (and the other archangels), and St. Thérèse of Lisieux. There are, of course, many other saints on the calendar, but we chose these six to celebrate with special recipes you'll find in the pages ahead.

Trinity Chicken Pot Pie

Every year on the Sunday after the Feast of Pentecost, the Church honors an important doctrine of our faith: the Trinity, which means that God is Father, Son, and Holy Spirit—three in one!

To celebrate this Feast of the Trinity, we are combining *three* elements that are the foundation of many wonderful dishes: onion, celery, and carrots. These ingredients together are called a "mirepoix," which will be the base for a festive pot pie!

Remember to ask for help from a grown-up whenever using the stove top or the oven.

Trinity Sunday
ORDINARY TIME

 DIFFICULT

SERVES: 6

PREPARATION:
1 hour

INGREDIENTS:
3 stalks of celery
3 carrots, peeled
1 onion
4 tablespoons butter
¾ cup frozen peas
2 cups cooked chicken (shredded or cut into small pieces)
1 cup all-purpose flour
2½ cups chicken broth
1 cup heavy cream
1 teaspoon ground thyme
2 teaspoons salt
¼ teaspoon black pepper
2 frozen pie crusts

SUPPLIES:
Large soup pot or Dutch oven
Pie pan

1. Preheat the oven to 400°F.

2. Dice your mirepoix (the celery, carrots, and onion).

3. Add the butter to a large soup pot and melt over medium heat. When the butter is melted, add the veggies (including the frozen peas) and sauté them in the butter for 5 minutes.

4. Add the chicken and flour and stir, then add the chicken broth and heavy cream. Turn down the heat to low and let the mixture cook for 5 minutes, then add your seasonings and turn off the heat.

5. Place one of your pie crusts into a pie pan and pour the chicken mixture into the pan. Place the second pie crust on top and pinch the sides together so that the mixture doesn't leak out while you're cooking it in the oven.

6. Bake between 30 and 40 minutes in the oven. The crust should turn golden brown but not be burnt. Carefully remove it from the oven and let it cool for a few minutes before serving!

Glory be to the Father
and to the Son
and to the Holy Spirit;
as it was in the beginning
is now, and ever shall be,
world without end.

Amen.

ARTWORK
Andrei Rublev
The Trinity
c. 1425

St. John the Baptist's Wild Honey Cake

St. John the Baptist was the cousin of Jesus, born to Elizabeth and Zechariah after they had prayed for many years to be blessed with a baby. God had a very important job for St. John the Baptist: preparing the way for Jesus by telling people that the Savior was coming and urging them to turn from their sins and get ready. John baptized many people (including Jesus!) in the Jordan River, which is why we call him St. John the *Baptist*. People may have thought John was very strange because he wore clothes made of camel hair and ate locusts and wild honey.

In honor of St. John the Baptist's eating habits, make a simple honey cake and top it with fresh fruit. (But don't worry—no locusts are involved!)

Nativity of St. John the Baptist

ORDINARY TIME | JUNE 24

 MODERATE

SERVES: 12

PREPARATION:
45 minutes

INGREDIENTS:
½ cup butter (softened)
1 cup honey
2 eggs
½ cup yogurt
1 teaspoon vanilla extract
2 cups flour
2 teaspoons baking powder
½ teaspoon salt

TOPPINGS:
Fresh fruit
Honey

SUPPLIES:
Cast iron skillet
Mixer

1. Preheat oven to 350°F.

2. Grease a cast iron skillet with butter.

3. In a mixing bowl, beat butter and honey until combined and then add the eggs one at a time. Add yogurt and vanilla.

4. In a separate bowl, mix the flour, baking powder, and salt, then add to the wet ingredients. Mix to combine.

5. Pour batter into cast iron skillet.

6. Bake in the oven for 30 to 35 minutes. You can tell if the cake is ready if a toothpick comes out clean.

7. Let the cake cool completely before adding your fresh fruit and drizzle of honey on the top, then serve!

In those days John the Baptist appeared in the wilderness of
Judea, proclaiming, "Repent, for the kingdom of heaven has
come near." This is the one of whom the prophet Isaiah spoke
when he said,

> *"The voice of one crying out in the wilderness:*
> *'Prepare the way of the Lord,*
> *make his paths straight.'"*

Now John wore clothing of camel's hair with a leather belt
around his waist, and his food was locusts and wild honey.
Then the people of Jerusalem and all Judea wre going out
to him, and all the region along the Jordan, and they were
baptized by him in the river Jordan, confessing their sins.

—MATTHEW 3:1–6

ARTWORK
Lippo Memmi
Saint John the Baptist
C. 1325

To the Heights Trail Mix

Pier Giorgio Frassati was an Italian youth who, like many young people, loved sports and the outdoors. But Frassati also had a heart for social justice and a deep Catholic faith that motivated his short life of social activism, opposition to fascism, care for the poor, and sacrifice for others. He died of an illness at age twenty-four, but his holiness continues to inspire us today.

Bl. Pier Giorgio Frassati loved God's beautiful creation. He enjoyed going *verso l'alto* or "to the heights" by leading hikes up in the mountains.

This simple but tasty trail mix is the perfect snack to take with you on a walk in the outdoors to honor this saintly hiker!

Bl. Pier Giorgio Frassati
ORDINARY TIME | JULY 4

 ● ◉ ◉ EASY

PREPARATION:
5 minutes

INGREDIENTS:
Peanuts
Cashews
Almonds
Raisins
M&Ms or chocolate chunks

1. Pour each ingredient into a large bowl.

2. Mix together with a large spoon and enjoy!

St. Charbel's Spicy Smashed Potatoes

St. Charbel Makhlouf was a Lebanese priest from the nineteenth century whose life of devotion to Jesus in the Blessed Sacrament inspired many people in his region. He was a *hermit*, a monk who lived in quiet solitude. St. Charbel was known for his intense discipline. He ate only once a day after saying his prayers. And he would often only eat vegetables, like boiled potato skins. After his death, his body was found to be perfectly preserved by the Lord, and many miracles occurred after prayers in front of his tomb. To celebrate his feast day, make these delicious and spicy Lebanese-inspired potatoes!

St. Charbel Makhlouf
ORDINARY TIME | JULY 24

 MODERATE

SERVES: 6

PREPARATION:
1 hour and 10 minutes

INGREDIENTS:
2 pounds small or mini potatoes
½ teaspoon baking soda
Olive oil
Salt
Pepper
10 cloves of minced garlic
1 teaspoon crushed coriander
½ teaspoon red pepper flakes
½ cup cilantro
The juice of 1 lemon

SUPPLIES:
Large pot
Colander
Baking sheet
Saucepan

1. Bring a large pot of water to a boil and add in the baking soda.

2. Boil the potatoes until fork-tender (about 15–30 minutes). Remove the pot from the heat and drain the potatoes with a colander. (You may need an adult to help as the water will be very hot.).

3. Preheat the oven to 400°F.

4. Lay the potatoes on a greased baking sheet and let them cool for 10 minutes (or until you can touch them without burning your fingers). Use the bottom of a glass to press them down flat.

5. Drizzle with olive oil and sprinkle with salt and pepper; bake for 25 to 30 minutes or until golden brown and crispy.

6. When the potatoes are almost finished, heat 2 tablespoons of olive oil in a saucepan over medium heat.

7. Add the minced garlic, red pepper flakes, and coriander. Stir and cook until fragrant (about 2 minutes).

8. Add the cilantro and lemon juice (to taste).

9. When the potatoes are done (and crispy!), toss them in the saucepan with the sauce and then put them back on the baking sheet to bake for another 5 minutes.

10. Sprinkle with the remaining cilantro and a pinch of salt and enjoy!

St. Hildegard's Cheerful Cookies

St. Hildegard of Bingen

ORDINARY TIME | SEPTEMBER 17

 ● ● ○ MODERATE

St. Hildegard was a German nun with extraordinary talents. She was a musician, composer, philosopher, mathematician, herbalist, and artist. When she was a little girl, she started seeing visions of God and was later encouraged to write down what she saw so that her visions could be shared with everyone. St. Hildegard became a feisty abbess and was one of the most famous women in all of Europe during her lifetime. Important people from near and far would write to her for advice. In 2012, Pope Benedict XVI declared her a Doctor of the Church—an honor given to only thirty-three men and four women—for making an extraordinary contribution to theology.

This is a very special recipe because it's actually based on a real recipe St. Hildegard included in one of her books about medicine and herbal remedies. St. Hildegard thought that the combination of spices in these tasty treats would bring joy to the heart. Give this recipe a try and see what you think!

SERVES: 6

PREPARATION:
30 minutes
(Plus 1 hour for chilling the dough)

INGREDIENTS:
¾ cup butter (1½ sticks, softened)
1 cup brown sugar
1 egg
1 teaspoon baking powder
¼ teaspoon salt
1½ cups flour
1 teaspoon ground cinnamon
½ teaspoon ground nutmeg
½ teaspoon ground cloves

SUPPLIES:
Stand or handheld mixer
Cookie sheet

1. Be sure to let your butter soften on the counter before you begin.

2. Add softened butter and brown sugar to a mixing bowl.

3. Cream the butter and brown sugar together, beating until the mixture is light and fluffy.

4. Add the egg and beat until combined with the butter and brown sugar.

5. Combine your dry ingredients (baking powder, salt, flour, cinnamon, nutmeg, and cloves) in a separate bowl.

6. Add half of this mixture to the wet ingredients and mix until combined. Then add the second half and mix.

7. Put your dough into the refrigerator for 1 hour.

8. Preheat your oven to 350°F.

9. Add 1-inch balls of dough onto a greased cookie sheet and then press them flat with the bottom of a cup.

10. Bake until the edges of the cookies are golden brown (about 12 to 15 minutes).

11. To achieve the floral design (pictured), we used a cookie press on the hot cookies to set the design before cooling. But this step is optional. Let your cheerful cookies cool for five minutes, then use a spatula to move them from the cookie sheet to a cooling rack or plate.

HILDEGARDIS *a Virgin Prophetess*, Abbeſs of
Sᵗ Rvperts Nunnerye. She died at Bingen Aº Do:
1180. Aged 82 yeares.

W. Marshall ſculpsit.

"O Eternal God, now may it please you
to burn in love
so that we become the limbs
fashioned in the love you felt
when you begot your Son
at the first dawn
before all creation.
And consider this need which falls upon us,
take it from us for the sake of your Son,
and lead us to the joy of your salvation."

—ST. HILDEGARD OF BINGEN

ARTWORK
W. Marshall
Hildegard von Bingen
UNKNOWN

St. Michael's Blackberry Crumble

The Archangels
ORDINARY TIME | SEPTEMBER 29

 MODERATE

This feast celebrates the archangels: St. Michael, St. Gabriel, and St. Raphael. Catholics traditionally prayed and fasted to thank God for his creation and the bounty of the earth during the "Ember Days" that fall just before this feast, and for many years, this feast day was referred to as "Michaelmas" or St. Michael's Mass.

In Hebrew, the name Michael means "Who is like God?" The answer, of course, is no one! This word "Michael" is the battle cry of the angels who fought against Lucifer and the fallen angels and defended the friends of God.

St. Gabriel announced the coming of Jesus to the Virgin Mary and also the birth of St. John the Baptist to Zechariah. His name means "God is my strength."

The story of St. Raphael is told in the book of Tobit, and his name means "God heals."

According to legend, when Lucifer was kicked out of heaven by St. Michael, he fell down into a thorny blackberry bush. He was so angry that he spit on the blackberries to make them bitter. This started the tradition of eating blackberries on Michaelmas in case the berries turned bitter afterwards!

"On Michaelmas Day the devil puts his foot on the blackberries."
—Irish Proverb

SERVES: 6

PREPARATION:
50 minutes

BLACKBERRY FILLING:
6 cups fresh or frozen blackberries
⅓ cup all-purpose flour
⅓ cup sugar

TOPPING:
⅔ cup old-fashioned oats
½ cup brown sugar
¼ cup all-purpose flour
4 tablespoons butter, softened
1 teaspoon ground cinnamon
¼ teaspoon salt
Optional: vanilla ice cream

SUPPLIES:
Baking dish
Bowl for mixing

1. Preheat your oven to 375°F.

2. Add blackberry filling ingredients to your baking dish and stir gently to combine.

3. In a bowl, add all the topping ingredients and mix. (You may have to use your hands.)

4. Add topping over the blackberry filling in your baking dish and spread it out evenly.

5. Bake for 40 minutes. You'll know your blackberry crumble is ready when the topping is golden brown and the blackberry filling is bubbling.

6. Have an adult help you remove the baking dish from the oven and let it cool for 15 minutes before serving (with vanilla ice cream if so desired).

Saint Michael the Archangel, defend us in battle.
Be our protection against the wickedness and snares of the devil.
May God rebuke him, we humbly pray;
and do thou, O Prince of the heavenly host,
by the power of God,
cast into hell Satan and all the evil spirits
who prowl about the world seeking the ruin of souls.

Amen.

ARTWORK
Andrei Rublev
Archangel Michael
1414

St. Thérèse's Favorite Chocolate Eclairs

St. Thérèse of Lisieux
ORDINARY TIME | OCTOBER 1

 ● ● ● DIFFICULT

"If every tiny flower wanted to be a rose, spring would lose its loveliness." —St. Thérèse of Lisieux

There are so many ways to be a saint. Saints might be martyrs, monks, missionaries, or evangelists. But they can also be ordinary people like you and me. St. Thérèse of Lisieux is a saint who reminds us that we can seek Jesus through "the Little Way" of small sacrifices and quiet love in our daily lives. Thérèse was a young girl in France who wanted nothing more than to live a life to glorify God. Thérèse became a nun at a very young age, and we can read her writings about learning to love Jesus through doing her chores well, loving her sisters even when it was difficult, and learning to pray.

As you learn about this little French saint, also called "the Little Flower," you may find you have a lot in common with Thérèse—especially if you have a sweet tooth! Thérèse loved her sweets (even though she didn't eat them in the convent), and when she was dying, her aunt even brought her some. Try making these chocolate eclairs, remembering Thérèse's favorite treat! Add dried rose petals if you like (remembering how this saint promised to send a "shower of roses" from heaven).

Note: This is a difficult recipe. You will need the help of a grown-up.

SERVES: 10

PREPARATION:

3.5 hours (3 hours for chilling the pastry cream in the fridge)

INGREDIENTS:

½ cup milk

½ cup unsalted butter

½ cup water

1 cup all-purpose flour

Pinch of salt

4 eggs

2 cups pastry cream (see ingredients for pastry cream below)

Optional: dried rose petals

CHOCOLATE GANACHE:

1 cup heavy whipping cream

1 bag chocolate chips

PASTRY CREAM:

½ cup sugar

¼ cup cornstarch

Pinch of kosher salt

2 tablespoons unsalted butter

4 large egg yolks

2 cups whole milk

1 teaspoon pure vanilla extract

SUPPLIES:

Medium bowl

Whisk

Parchment paper

Metal piping tip

Baking sheet

Saucepan

St. Thérèse's Favorite Chocolate Eclairs (Continued)

MAKING THE PASTRY CREAM

1. In a medium bowl, add sugar, cornstarch, and salt and set aside.

2. Melt the butter on a saucepan over medium heat. Once melted, reduce the heat slightly. Whisk together the egg yolks and milk and pour into a saucepan on low to medium heat. Immediately add the sugar, cornstarch, and salt mixture to the saucepan and stir continuously until thickened. It takes several minutes for the mixture to thicken. Don't get discouraged; just keep stirring, and all of a sudden it will thicken. You know it's thick enough when your whisk leaves trails in the mixture and it becomes harder to stir.

3. Remove the mixture from the heat, pour into a bowl, and stir in the vanilla extract.

4. Cover the top of the mixture with wax paper, parchment paper, or plastic wrap, and let it cool for 20 minutes before transferring to the fridge.

5. Let chill for at least 3 hours.*

MAKING THE ECLAIRS

1. Heat a saucepan on the stove over medium heat.

2. Add the milk, butter, and water to the saucepan, stirring until the butter has melted.

3. Increase the heat until just boiling, then remove from heat immediately.

4. Add the flour and a pinch of salt, stirring continuously until the mixture is smooth, doesn't stick to the pan, and looks like mashed potatoes.

5. Add the eggs to the mixture and stir continuously over low–medium heat until it has a paste-like consistency.

6. Remove from heat and allow to cool.

7. Preheat the oven to 400°F.

8. Fold parchment paper into a piping cone and cut off the tip.

9. Line baking sheets with parchment paper.

10. Fill the piping cone with the mixture and pipe a 3-cm-long length of the dough (1-inch wide).**

11. Bake for 15 minutes, then remove and allow the pastries to fully cool.

12. Make another parchment paper piping bag and insert a metal tip.

13. Fill the piping bag with pastry cream. To fill the eclairs, poke three holes with your piping tip into the bottom of the eclair and fill with pastry cream. Set aside to rest.

14. Pour the chocolate chips into a heat-proof bowl and set aside.

15. Add the heavy whipping cream to a saucepan over medium heat.

16. Stirring occasionally, heat until the cream simmers at the edges. (Be sure not to boil.).

17. Remove from heat and pour over the chocolate, whisking until smooth.

18. Dip your eclairs into the chocolate, add the optional dried rose petals on top, and set aside for cooling.

If making in advance, the cream will keep for up to 2 days in the fridge.

**Leave room for the eclair to bubble up.*

"Jesus, allow me to save very many souls; let no soul be lost today; let all the souls in purgatory be saved. Jesus, pardon me if I say anything I should not say. I want only to give you joy and to console you."

—ST. THÉRÈSE OF LISIEUX

ARTWORK
Blair Barlow
Little Flower
2022

Hallowtide

On October 31st, families celebrate Halloween, but many don't know that this festive day began as a Catholic holy day. The word "Halloween" is an abbreviation of "All Hallows Eve," the night before All Saints Day. "Hallow" is an old-fashioned word for "saint" or "holy." Just think of the Our Father prayer, when we say "hallowed be thy name" (holy is your name).

On All Saints Day, November 1st, we celebrate every saint in heaven and we remember that God wants us to join him in paradise with these holy men and women. The saints in heaven give us hope and remind us that we are called to be saints like them. The next day is All Souls Day (November 2nd), and all together, these three days are called Hallowtide.

Whatever your family's traditions are for Halloween, you can use these special days to celebrate the saints in heaven and pray for all the souls in purgatory.

Soul Cakes

All Souls

ORDINARY TIME | NOVEMBER 2

 MODERATE

All Souls Day, celebrated in some parts of the world as Día de los Muertos, is a day when we remember those who have died and pray for their souls. It's a time to remember loved ones and family members who have passed away and to intercede for them. You can even visit a local cemetery and pray for the people who are buried there. This might sound spooky or unsettling, but remember that the day before All Souls Day is All Saints Day. This important time in the Christian year reminds us that when we die, we have the hope of the Resurrection! We don't have to view death with fear because Christ has conquered death.

Did you know that the modern-day practice of trick-or-treating for Halloween first developed when people would go door-to-door singing and asking for little breads called soul cakes? In exchange for a snack, they would say prayers for those who had died.

SERVES: 6

PREPARATION:
30 minutes

INGREDIENTS:
1 stick butter
1 cup sugar
3 egg yolks
3 cups self-rising flour
½ teaspoon allspice
1 teaspoon cinnamon
½ teaspoon ginger
¼ teaspoon clove
¼ teaspoon nutmeg
8 tablespoons milk
½ cup raisins
Optional: powdered sugar to add on top

SUPPLIES:
Baking sheet
Parchment paper
Rolling pin
Mixer

1. Preheat oven to 375°F.

2. Line baking sheet with parchment paper.

3. Add butter and sugar to the mixer and and mix them together until smooth

4. Add egg yolks and beat mixture.

5. Add flour, spices, then milk and mix.

6. Roll out the dough on a lightly floured surface and cut out circles with a cookie cutter or the top of a cup.

7. Add raisins to the top and then bake in the oven until golden brown. (Check after 10 minutes.)

A soul! a soul! a soul-cake!
Please good Missis, a soul-cake!
An apple, a pear, a plum, or a cherry,
Any good thing to make us all merry.
One for Peter, two for Paul
Three for Him who made us all.

—TRADITIONAL CHILDREN'S SONG

Christ the King Breakfast Crowns

Each November, the Church celebrates the Feast of Christ the King. This feast day reminds us that no matter what country or culture we come from, we are all united under the rule of Jesus Christ. He is the King of the entire universe. This is an important feast day because it reminds us to practice our faith in public, not just at home!

For this feast day, celebrate by making these Christ the King breakfast crowns. These delectable one-bite breakfast foods are meant to be shared, so think about how you can bring this meal and the message of the day to the poor and vulnerable of your community.

Christ the King
ORDINARY TIME

● ● ○ **MODERATE**

SERVES: 6

PREPARATION:
1 hour

INGREDIENTS:
12 slices of bacon
1 cup frozen hashbrowns
Garlic salt
12 slices of bread
1 dozen eggs
¾ cup milk
Salt
Pepper
1 cup shredded cheddar cheese

SUPPLIES:
Muffin tin
Drinking glass
Pan

1. Thoroughly grease a muffin tin. (The egg will cling to any spots that haven't been greased.)

2. Heat a pan on the stove over medium heat and cook the bacon (until cooked but not crisp).

3. Remove the bacon and set aside. Cook the hashbrowns in the remaining bacon grease and season with garlic salt. Wait until the hashbrowns are cooked but not crisp, then set them on paper towel to drain the grease.

4. Using a glass, cut circles out of the pieces of bread about the size of the muffin tin base.

5. Preheat the oven to 375°F.

6. Place the circles of bread in the center of each muffin tin.

7. Wrap 1 piece of bacon around the sides of the muffin tin and layer hashbrowns on top of the bread.

8. In a bowl, whisk together the eggs and milk and season with salt and pepper.

9. Pour the egg mixture into each muffin tin.

10. Sprinkle cheddar cheese over each egg.

11. Place the muffin tin in the oven and bake for 25 minutes. Let cool for 5 minutes and enjoy!

Crown him with many crowns,
  the Lamb upon his throne;
Hark! how the heavenly anthem drowns
  all music but its own:
Awake, my soul, and sing
  of him who died for thee,
and hail him as thy matchless king
  through all eternity.

—"CROWN HIM WITH MANY CROWNS"

ARTWORK
Unknown
Christ Pantocrator
SIXTH CENTURY

It Begins Again

The beauty of the liturgical year is that we get to experience it again and again. It slowly forms us, teaches us, and helps us lift our hearts to God. As this year ends and a new season of Advent begins, consider how you've grown in faith, hope, and love over the past twelve months, and ask God to continue drawing you closer to him in the year to come.

Haley Stewart

Haley Stewart is the Editor of Word on Fire Votive and the award-winning author of several books for grown-ups and some for young readers, including a series about mouse nuns called *The Sister Seraphina Mysteries*. She lives in Florida with her husband and four kids, who all love to cook.

Clare Sheaf

Clare Sheaf is a designer and photographer for Word on Fire. She loves to create from her home in Texas where she lives with her husband, Jacob, and her daughter, Annie.

Acknowledgments

Special thanks to the Fredrickson family for sharing your kitchen, creativity, and delightful children with us as we photographed these recipes. Marisa, your culinary expertise and food styling talents were invaluable. Nash, Rio, Shepherd, and Matej, your enthusiasm, helpfulness, and cooking skills made this project a delight. Nic, as with every Votive project, your visual genius and fresh ideas made this book beautiful. Thanks also to the sweet Lydia and her mother Beth for modeling. And thank you to our families for letting us test so many recipes on you!

References

p. 41

Prayer from "The Little Office of St. Nicholas," St. Nicholas Center website, stnicholascenter.org.

p. 70

Recipe inspired by K.C. Cornwell's Traditional Sugar Plums Recipe for G-FreeFoodie.com.

p. 74

Recipe inspired by Barbara Schieving's Quick Mardi Gras King Cake for BettyCrocker.com.

p. 93

Paul Miki, quoted in Carol Kelly-Gangi, *365 Days with the Saints: A Year of Wisdom from the Saints* (New York: Wellfleet, 2015), 27.

p. 100

Recipe inspired by John Kanell's Artisan Bread for preppykitchen. com.

p. 109

Pius IX, quoted in Thomas H. Kinane, *St. Joseph: His Life, His Virtues, His Privileges, His Power* (Dublin: M.H. Gill, 1884), 273.

p. 137

The Golden Legend; or, Lives of the Saints, ed. Jacobus de Voragine, trans. William Caxton ([1265] 1483).

p. 141

Catherine of Siena, quoted in Merridith Frediani, "7 Quotes from St. Catherine of Siena," Ascension, April 26, 2019, https://media.ascensionpress. com/2019/04/26/7-quotes-from-st-catherine-of-siena/.

p. 146

Recipe inspired by Scott and Chris's Easy French Almond Cake for thecafesucrefarine.com.

p. 158

Recipe inspired by Ree Drummond's Chicken Pot Pie for The Pioneer Woman.

p. 177

Hildegard of Bingen, "O Eterne Deus," in *Selected Writings*, trans. Mark Atherton (London: Penguin, 2005), ebook.

p. 184

Recipe inspired by Missy Wombat's Chocolate Eclairs for food.com and by Joy the Baker's Small-Batch Chocolate Eclairs for joythebaker. com.

p. 189

Thérèse of Lisieux, "A Letter Sister Thérèse Carried on Her Heart on the Day of Her Profession," September 8, 1890, in *Story of a Soul: The Autobiography of Saint Thérèse of Lisieux*, trans. John Clarke (Park Ridge, IL: Word on Fire Classics, 2022), 277.

p. 201

Matthew Bridges and Godfrey Thring, "Crown Him with Many Crowns," 1851, hymnary.org.